CW00765134

S/4
2. 00

Minor Field Sports

By

L. C. R. CAMERON

Author of *The Wild Foods of Great Britain,*
Otters & Otter Hunting, etc.

ILLUSTRATED

LONDON
GEORGE ROUTLEDGE & SONS, LTD.
NEW YORK: E. P. DUTTON & CO.

PREFACE

IT is greatly to be feared that, with the increased and ever-increasing cost of every form of country sport and its accessories, the youth of the future can scarcely look forward to having such a "good time" as did their fathers and elder brothers. Not for the sons of the "new poor" are the ponies that took their predecessors to meets of the hounds ; nor, perhaps, the gun or the rifle with which the keeper taught them to shoot the sitting rabbit. Not for them, either, the joy of fishing with a fly-rod, now that the "newly-rich" from the manufacturing centres are flocking in their thousands to the streams and brooks of the most remote parts of the country, to lease the fishing rights and supplant the local sportsman.

The boy of the future whose lines are cast in country places will have, figuratively speaking, to cut his sports-coat according to a very short measure of cloth. Nevertheless, to the youth of the right stamp, rightly instructed, there still remains a heritage of many Minor Field Sports, that may pleasurably and profitably fill his days, and add to his stock of natural knowledge ; in addition to providing him with good health and a store of memories that shall last him, perhaps, long after the power or desire of enjoying any form of sport shall have vanished away.

It is to bring such inexpensive forms of sport to the notice of youths and boys who have possibly lost (as have, alas ! so many) their natural instructors in such matters, in the persons of fathers, uncles, and big brothers killed in the war, that this book has been conceived. There are few country boys who cannot compass a dog of some sort ; and with a useful dog much may be done. Ferrets, too, although dearer than they once were, should be within the reach of most boys, and they can be made to pay for their keep ; while there are certain sporting birds to be procured at small expense, out of which great fun is to be obtained.

For the rest, the book will show how much healthy and genuine sport in a small way is to be had by those who will be content to make and use their own implements of the chase ; for which sufficient directions are given in clear and simple language, supplemented when necessary by illustrations.

It is not every boy who possesses a bent for games, nor is it always good that boys should be occupied with the organised games of the school playing-field to the neglect of sports and pastimes that take them into the heart of the country and place them in contact with Nature : which must always remain the same, whatever the changes man may make in the conditions of life and in its more serious aspects. Also, there are many boys who do not possess the requisite number of companions in and around their homes to render the playing of games at all practicable. But with a dog, a ferret, a kit of pigeons, or a trained

sparrow-hawk, together with that instinct for
true sport which it is the aim of this book to
inculcate, such lonely boys may yet find healthy
occupation and amusement, which for lack of
such a teacher they might very likely chance to
miss.

At a time when the best prospects of at least
the boy already at school would appear to lie in
lands remote from Britain, the pursuit of these
Minor Field Sports at home must inevitably
prove a valuable training for the life that may
await him beyond the seas.

Lastly, there may be sportsmen " of a larger
growth,"—no longer able to pursue the field
sports that were once their joy, by reason of
increased cost, coupled possibly with a reduced
income—who will welcome a guide to less expensive but not less genuine sports ; and be glad
to find recreation, in default of better, in the
pursuit of the quite " small deer " of the chase :
to " seek for health on the windy hill and wisdom
too."

L. C. R. C.

Radnor Forest.

LIST OF ILLUSTRATIONS

FULL-PAGE PLATES

CONTENTS

Minor Field Sports

INTRODUCTORY

IT is necessary in the first place to say something of the principles which must actuate the man or boy who, in the pursuit of his natural instinct to find recreation among the beasts and birds of the field, aspires to win for himself the title of Sportsman : the most honourable title that it is possible for any human being to bear, since it cannot be conferred except by the universal suffrage of his peers, and can only be earned by the consistent observance of laws that are for the most part unwritten, but have alike their origin and their sanction in quite the best qualities of human nature.

The difference between a Sportsman and a " Sporting Man " is so great that there is practically no resemblance between them. A poacher may be a " sporting man," but never a sportsman. The two chief characteristics of a poacher are, first, his complete disregard of his duty towards

A

his neighbour, and, second, his total denial of law to the game ; and it is precisely the observance of these two points of conduct that constitutes the quality which is recognized as Sportsmanship. Without them, skill and craftsmanship, knowledge of wild life, even courage and power of endurance, avail nothing : they will, alone, never make a man a sportsman : just as a knowledge of languages will not make a man a diplomatist, nor skill in fencing or shooting render him a capable soldier.

If this fact be borne in mind it will follow that, no matter how comparatively insignificant the quarry pursued, or how primitive the implements of chase employed, indulgence in the minor field sports dealt with in these pages will prove not less honourable than the enjoyment of those more important and expensive sports, whose records are published periodically in books, magazines, and newspapers for the admiration and entertainment of their readers.

The young follower of such minor sports as ratting and crayfish-catching, hawking blackbirds, or ferreting rabbits, must learn that he and the pleasure he legitimately derives from their pursuit must be the final, and not the first consideration to be aimed at. There are many considerations to be taken into account before these.

First and foremost comes the point whether his sport will in anyway interfere with that of his neighbour or do any kind of harm to the interests of other people and their property. If it will, it is no longer sportsmanlike. Thus to wire pike in a stream where angling for these fish is practised, is unsportsmanlike; but in a river where trout and grayling only are required, and pike regarded as vermin, the wiring or even grappling for these fresh-water sharks becomes a genuine sport, which no one need be ashamed to pursue if he possess the necessary right or has obtained permission to do so.

A true sportsman will never trespass upon nor run the risk of damaging the property of anyone of whom he has obtained permission to go upon his land or his water. If accidental damage occur—and in sport, as in life, accidents will happen—it should be immediately repaired: a gap in a hedge at once be made-up, or steps retraced to close a gate that may have blown open after use, through being carelessly fastened.

Dogs should not be taken through fields where ewes and lambs, or in-lamb ewes, are pastured; nor allowed to enter coverts where game-birds are sitting or into which young pheasants have been turned. A terrier should not be taken along the banks of a stream in search of water-voles or moor-hens when the visit of a pack of otter-hounds to the water is impending. Pigeons should not be loosed from their lofts when farmers are sowing their grain : nor when they can damage the gardener's crop of peas. These are only a few of the countless matters that must engage the attention of the youth who aspires to prove himself a sportsman. If he does not learn to think first and most of others he will never earn the title.

Again he must strictly observe the laws and bye-laws, the regulations as to times and seasons, made by the community—whether national or local—of which he chances to be a member ; and this in his own as well as in the general interest. He must not carry a gun or own a dog unless he possesses a license to do so ; nor ever take a fish during the close season ; nor rob a bird of its entire clutch of eggs, however common the species may be or however valuable the eggs. To do otherwise were to brand himself as a poacher, and might indicate the possession of other undesirable tendencies, common to pro-fessional poachers, towards drunkenness, idleness, cruelty to animals, and even wife-beating, theft and other criminal attributes, which characterize all poachers with few exceptions, despite the misguided efforts of some ill-informed writers to set them in a falsely romantic light.

The true sportsman is always humane, even to his quarry; and even when that quarry is vermin, which has to be destroyed wholesale lest it damage property of more real value than itself: as do rats and sparrows, to name none other. If anything has to be killed it must be killed as quickly and painlessly as possible, and never allowed to suffer unnecessarily for an instant. Thus a fish should be killed directly it is grassed, a wounded bird or rabbit put out of its pain the moment it is retrieved. Nothing living should be kept in suspense or the possibility of fear for the mere purpose of causing " amusement ": there is no real " amusement " in it for a true sportsman.

If the captured quarry is to be retained for any purpose, as a sparrow-hawk for hawking, or minnows for live-bait, their well-being must come before that of their temporary owners. It is the same with dogs, or ferrets. No boy should be permitted to break his fast of a morning until he has cleaned and fed and watered his

live-stock ; and after a day's sport the owner
of ferret or dog or pony should, before seeing to
his own wants or even changing out of his wet
things, himself see that the animals that have
ministered to his enjoyment are first made comfortable. No servant should be permitted to do
this, and even if a groom cleans the pony its
rider should stand by and see it done, and feed
the pony himself after riding him. The reward
will be great in more ways than one : since no
animal will do its best work for him who does not
feed and care for it, and whom in this way it
insensibly learns to trust and depend upon, and
for whom it will very soon be willing to do anything in its power, out of gratitude for the benefits
it receives at his hands.

All animals hunted to destruction—as distinguished from those sought in order to be made
use of alive, such as sparrow-hawks, jackdaws,
and magpies—with the exception only of noxious
vermin—must be allowed a sporting chance
of escape. In terms of the Turf this may be
stated as the odds of " 3 to 1 on " its escaping
uninjured. Only in shooting will it prove difficult
to provide that these odds shall be maintained ;
but here the effort must be made. This is best
done by arming a boy with a rook- or rabbit-

rifle, since if a bird or beast is struck by the bullet it is generally killed. If a shot-gun is used it should be a double-barrelled one, and its user should be taught to fire the second barrel at once if a bird is obviously hit but does not fall. The boy should be taught that the one aim in shooting must be to kill the bird in the air so that it falls to the ground dead. No man who cannot do this at least nine times out of ten with one or other barrel of his gun can be called a good shot : and no man unable to count upon doing so who continues to shoot at and maim birds has any claim to the honoured title of sportsman. In the tenth case, where the bird falls wounded to the ground and becomes a runner, the sportsman should at once, with or without the aid of a dog, set to work to find the wounded bird and bring it to hand ; nor should he fire at any other game until he has succeeded in doing so.

It is to be feared that very few of the men who have recently become, and are in the future increasingly likely to become, the owners or lessees of English shootings, and still fewer of the gamekeepers whom they employ, will come within the above definition of sportsmen. They have invented an alleged sporting code of their

own ; and consider that no man who does not
pay at least £1 an acre for his shooting, or £100
a mile for his dry-fly water, has any right to
enjoy any kind of field-sport, however minor ;
much less to carry a gun or wield a fly-rod.
Circumstances, of course, differ in different
parts of the country : and some places are more
favoured than others. Still, it is pretty certain
that the boys and youths for whose benefit this
book is chiefly written are more likely to be
hampered in their enjoyment by tenants and
keepers of this type than by anybody else. These
" sporting men " are pretty sure to regard them
as poachers, because they or their people are not
rich ; and the keepers will take every chance
of calumniating them to their employers, if only
as a convenient way of concealing their own
delinquencies. Should a boy, inadvertently—
through excitement or from some other cause—
kill anything he has no right to kill, my advice
to him—whether he thinks he has been seen by
a keeper or watcher or not : a thing he can never
be certain about—is to go straight to the owner,
taking the quarry with him, and confess the fact.
He can hardly be disbelieved under such circumstances ; and will have his own reward, in any
case, in knowing that he has done the sportsman-

like thing. If the owner against whom he has
offended happens to possess the true instincts
of a sportsman the reward of the honest offender
will certainly be greater. However, in this book,
shooting will occupy but little space, though it
must be given some ; and the point need not be
laboured here.

Another thing to which the young sportsman
must, in order to qualify for the title, attend
personally, is the care of his implements of the
chase. He must clean his own gun or rifle, oil
his otter-pole, wash his rabbit-nets, brush and
polish his dog-collars, and in fact keep all his
weapons always in order. He ought, in fact, to
dubbin his own shoes, and it were no bad thing if
he learnt to darn neatly or to put a sightly patch
upon such garments as he may tear in the pursuit
of sport. Directions are given under various
sections as to how such things as traps and nets,
wires, jesses, lures, and such-like can be made
at home ; and the need for personal attention to
dogs, ferrets, and birds, so that they may be kept
in health, free from vermin, and in equal comfort
to that enjoyed by their masters, has already
been emphasized. Just as a genius has been
defined as a man with an infinite capacity for
taking pains, so a sportsman cannot be considered

perfect unless he has mastered all the minutiæ of his hobbies. However well-off and however well-served he may be destined to become, he will never regret knowing how things should be done ; and if, as he should with advantages of education and intellect, he can do things better himself, then he will be even better served by his employees.

The boy who follows the precepts laid down throughout the whole of this little volume can hardly fail—if he is the boy I take him for—to turn into a genuine sportsman ; and by following these minor sports without offence to his neighbour, injustice to his quarry, injury to his sporting pets or damage to his accessories, will fit himself well and truly to bear his part, when and if the opportunity shall come, in the major field sports of Hunting, Hawking, Coursing, Fishing, and Shooting, in whatever part of the habitable world his lot may eventually be cast.

If such opportunity should never come, well, he will still have his minor sports to occupy his leisure hours, provided that as a sportsman he constrains himself to accept them in the true spirit of that mediæval Latin grace : *Benedic Domine dona tua, qui de tua largitate summus sumpturis.*

I : SPORTS DEPENDING CHIEFLY ON DOGS

PRELIMINARY NOTES

THE most important question for the boy who intends going in for one of the minor sports enlisted under this heading is : What sort of dog shall I own ? especially if he can afford to keep but one. The list of suitable dogs is not a long one. It comprises terriers of various sorts, beagles, spaniels, whippets, and cross-bred dogs between any two of these breeds. The cross-bred dog is not a " mongrel " : it is only when one cross-bred dog interbreeds with another that the mongrel appears, if the two parents represent three or four breeds between them. The breeding of mongrels should not be permitted ; but a cross-bred dog is often a very clever, intelligent animal, and one that will prove a most serviceable companion for the one-dog minor sportsman.

Such dogs are often to be purchased as puppies for a few shillings, even to-day ; and no one can hope to get the best out of a dog unless he acquires him when a puppy. Like women, dogs are very faithful to their first loves, and their first master's whistle will usually recall them even after many years. Like women, too, it is often only after they have changed hands several times that they settle down to the real lasting affection of their lives and discover who their true masters are, those whom they can absolutely trust and in whose companionship,they can be really happy. So that a dog should be caught young, or else bought after it has passed through several changes of ownership. In either case they should not prove very expensive to buy or to keep.

According to the sport for which it is required, so must the dog be selected. If badger-hunting be the sport, a bull-terrier, or a cross-bred dog having bull-terrier blood on one side, should be chosen. Such a dog is, however, of very little use for other sports, while most dogs will hunt a badger ; and in any case this is not a very important minor sport, as it is not everywhere that badgers are found, nor are all boys allowed out at night to hunt them. If intended to hunt the stoat, beagles will be necessary or a beagle-terrier cross-bred. Highland terriers (now called Cairn terriers and rapidly losing their sporting character under the deteriorating influence of the show-bench) are also good at stoat-hunting, and excellent for catching water-voles and moor-hens. A fox-terrier-spaniel cross-bred is also good for the latter bird, as for rabbiting and finding

White West Highland Terrier.

Cocker Spaniel.

[*Face p.* 12.

FOX TERRIER.

BEAGLE.

[*Face p.* 13.

hedgehogs, and the spaniel, of course, is good for all shooting purposes. For wild rabbit-coursing and dog-racing the whippet and terrier-and-whippet cross-bred are indicated. Fox-terriers—the doubtful sort—are good for hunting most things, and share with the Highland terrier a fondness for killing rats that is ineradicable.

The Irish terrier is a quarrelsome dog, generally useless for any sporting purpose, and the Welsh terrier is usually too small and soft to be of much use ; but the Border terrier is a game little beast and good at many things. Most dogs can be taught to " hunt the clean boot," a sport usually reserved for bloodhounds. I had a Highland terrier called " Biodag " that would hunt a trail 15 minutes old for upwards of two miles : and would go to ground to fox, otter, or badger, catch water-voles and moor-hens, kill rats, rabbits and stoats, and once won five heats at a rabbit-coursing meeting : a dog of a sort hard to come by.

The young sportsman must, therefore, make his choice, or take the first likely " hound " that offers at a reasonable price. If, as is most likely, the dog has latent good qualities, it is up to his owner to bring them out. A fool of a dog has usually a fool for a master—or mistress.

Whatever the breed or cross-bred chosen, the making or marring of the individual specimen thereof must always lie with its owner. He should from the very start have absolute control of the animal, even to fetching it from its previous owner and letting it see the money paid over for it. Dogs understand such things. Then he should himself take it home and introduce it to its new surroundings, not dragging it along, if it should prove reluctant, but carrying it (if a puppy or small enough) and if not, taking it in some conveyance. It is most important to create a good impression on it at the very beginning.

The first thing to do with a new dog on getting it home is to give it food and water, and a definite place close to the latter as a bed. In order to get the best out of a dog it should be closely associated in companionship with its master; and, therefore, wherever possible, should live in the house. I would go farther and assign it a sleeping place in his bedroom. But it must never be foolishly petted, pampered, or treated like a lap-dog. The floor is good enough for a dog, but the place where it lies should not be draughty nor should it be in front of or close to a fire. At meal-times the dog should be under the table. No dog should be fed at the same time as human beings are feeding, nor given even the smallest scrap ; and no dog intended for sporting purposes should be taught " parlour tricks."

A dog's diet should be simple and sufficient. Half a biscuit, according to age and size, should be offered it dry, in the morning : if refused it should be taken away and the dog not allowed to bury it in the garden or hide it under a sofa-cushion. Its only other meal should be dinner, given some time between 4 and 6 o'clock—as near 5 o'clock as possible. This should consist of a little cooked meat, green vegetables—cooked " stinging nettles " will do—soaked crust of bread or broken biscuit, and thin warm gravy. It should be varied, soaked dog-meal being given one day instead of meat, or even bread-crusts in gravy or Bovril, or oatmeal and broth. Fish, potatoes, cheese, and milk should never be given to any dog intended to be used as a sporting companion, nor any sweet food such as biscuits, cake, or sweetmeats. As a reward for obedience during early training a bit of raw meat or a lump of sugar may be given sparingly. If a dog does not finish his meal the dish should be promptly removed : it should never be permitted to " cut and come again " at will.

If a dog cannot for any reason be accommodated indoors it should be given a bed in a loose-box or snug out-house, or provided with a kennel surrounded with an enclosure of railings, palings, or wire-netting. No dog should ever be placed on a chain : indeed the placing of dogs on chains should be made illegal. A kennel should be cleaned out and the bedding in winter changed every day *by the dog's owner*. Wherever a dog sleeps there should his water-trough be, and it should be accessible to the animal at all times. The water should be fresh every morning—in the summer-time in the evening also—and should never stand in the sun. A pinch of flowers of sulphur (not rock sulphur) should always be cast into the water-trough, and a pinch also given with the dinner all through the warm months of the year. All dogs must have access to growing grass, and must be exercised every day.

Patience is all that is required in the actual training of a dog, whether to be clean in a house or useful in the field. It should never be told to do a thing unless it is seriously intended to be made to do it : and it is hopeless to encourage a dog to do a thing one day and to forbid it the next. There is one thing a dog cannot understand, clever as he may be and generally is, and that is inconsistency.

Dogs, like children, will require occasional punishment, but they should never be punished in hot anger, and they must never be struck with a stick. If a dog-whip is not handy, the palm of the hand should be used : even a piece of rope or cord, or a leathern strap is preferable to a stick. The punishment must follow hard upon the discovery of the fault or it will be useless, as the dog will not know for what fault he is punished.

The chief things to teach a dog intended for sporting purposes is to come to the voice or whistle, to wait at heel under any temptation, and to remain there until released by its master's signal. This is its elementary or squad drill : the rest of its training, whether to go to ground, retrieve, course a rabbit or what not, depends on its breed, and is merely in the nature of developing its natural instincts. These will inevitably manifest themselves at the proper time, provided the ordinary training be correctly and patiently carried out, and the animal taught by the following of the above simple rules to trust and place unbounded confidence in its owner. Except these simple rules be followed there can be little

B

hope of any sportsman, young or old, getting the best work out of his dogs.

Hints on special training and entering to various forms of minor sport will be given under each sub-section.

1. BADGER-HUNTING

I have placed this minor sport first because the badger is the largest and most formidable quarry with which the boy-sportsman is likely to have dealings. But otherwise it is not a very important form of the chase : partly because it is not everywhere that it can be pursued and partly because it must be followed by moonlight. All sorts of dogs may be employed, from an old fox-hound to a sheep-dog, but only a bull-terrier is really capable of overtaking and holding a badger until "the field " arrive to sack or despatch it.

The plan of operations is to set out shortly, before midnight on a bright moonlight night and draw the meadows within a mile or so of a " sett " or earth known to be tenanted by a family of badgers. The quarry will be found by the dogs —of course several must be used—roaming about in search of hedgehogs, young rabbits, mice, rats and the other articles in this truly omni-verous mammal's dietary, and will at once set off at an incredibly brisk pace for its " sett ". The dogs should give tongue as a signal to the field that the quarry is before them ; and it then becomes a race for the place of refuge. If the dogs overtake the badger before it reaches the "sett," they ought to hold it until the " field "come up ; when, if required to be taken alive " for export," it can be " tailed " by some expert at that game and popped into a sack ; or, if its death is sought to be encompassed, a smart blow on the snout, its only vulnerable spot, will promptly render it unconscious. Its capture may be made more secure if the entrances to the " sett " are previously stopped with sacks furnished with running nooses in which the badger entraps itself. If this be not done it is unwise to take out small terriers accustomed to go to ground ; as if the badger succeeds in getting home they will follow it in and perhaps get killed or lost.

2. STOAT-HUNTING

This, in contradistinction to badger-hunting, is an early morning pursuit like otter-hunting, the stoat, like the otter, having to be found by its overnight " drag." Small 12-inch beagles, terriers, and beagle-terrier cross-breds are the hounds or dogs for this sport, which is one of the prettiest of all minor sports ; and in these days, owing to the enormous increase in these vicious little vermin during the absence of game-keepers at the War, one of the most immediately useful.

Except in April, May, and early June, a country that is chiefly arable is not very suitable to stoat-hunting owing to the possibility of damage to growing crops. In highly-preserved country, too, although it is precisely here that stoats are most numerous, stoat-hunters will not be popular, owing to nesting game-birds. The best " countries " are what are known as " stone-wall countries "; for stoats like to lie up in dry-stone walls and are thence easily dislodged. The same applies to wild rough, hilly countries, where cairns and clitters of rocks abound ; though here the dislodging part of the business is not so easy.

In all countries the methods to be pursued are practically identical. Starting soon after dawn with two or three couples of beagles and terriers the quarry is drawn for in such likely places as round a farm-yard, a rabbit-warren, an outlying hen-house in a meadow or stubble-field, and (where permission has been obtained) round about coverts where pheasants abound. Sooner or later the " pack " will hit off the morning drag of the stoat that has been prowling about in search of eggs, or chicks, or bunnies, and will go off at score in full cry like a miniature pack of hounds. The quarry may have travelled a mile or more before going to bed for the day : if it should chance to be the drag of a " trip " or family of stoats it may be much farther ; but there will be all the more fun when " hounds " mark. The next trouble will be to dislodge the quarry. If it be from a loose dry-stone wall it will not be difficult to pull sufficient of it away to get the stoat to shift his quarters : always remembering to replace the stones. A spade will often be required for hedge-banks and perhaps a crowbar for roots of trees. Fortunately the stoat has an inveterate hatred of tobacco, and a big-bowled long-stemmed pipe is one of the necessary implements of this form of the chase. It should be half-filled with strong tobacco, lighted, the stem introduced into the hole at which hounds have marked, and the smoke blown into the retreat ; any adjacent apertures through which the smoke can escape being stopped up with clods of earth. The " pack " will, meantime, have been taken to a little distance under the charge

of the " Master " of the moment. In a very
brief time the stoat will emerge, and the man
with the pipe will have to look sharp that it doesn't
fasten on him : I once saw the " tobacconist "
nipped by the nose in this way. Once clear,
the stoat will go off at a surprising pace, and in
a fairly open country a little law may be allowed
before the " pack " is laid on. The run proper
then commences, and great fun it is, stoats
having been known on rare occasions to stand up
before beagles for as many as four miles. Stoats
are like most of the weasel tribe, great wanderers
and acquainted with a large extent of country and
many diverse " holts," and appear always to
make for some stronger place of refuge than that
from which they have just been evicted. It
takes good hounds and terriers to overtake
them, and " the field " must be able to go on a bit
as well. A hunting-horn—one of the Köhler reed-
horns is advisable, since it is often rather a breath-
less sport—should be carried by the " Master "
and small crops used to keep the " pack " together
and under control. Altogether this minor sport
approximates most closely to the " real sport "
of hunting than any other, and deserves the attention of that " sportsman of a larger growth " of
whom I have spoken in my preface. The boy

who can kill a brace or leash of stoats before breakfast has every right to be justly proud of his achievement, and can never have a better chance of showing his prowess than during the next few years.

Where a boy cannot himself afford to keep a sufficient number of beagles or beagle-terriers for stoat-hunting he should persuade some of his young compeers in the same district to keep one or two apiece, and to bring them along to a " meet " on stated days, on the principle of the trencher-fed packs of fox-hounds of bygone days. Their owners must be careful not to feed their little " hounds " late on the day before an intended hunt : the full meal must be given in the morning, and the half-biscuit at night on these occasions ; and they should be fed and " kennelled-up " on their return from hunting.

3. RAT-HUNTING

The eighth Duke of Beaufort is reputed to have said that there were only two sports, fox-hunting and rat-hunting, and that rat-hunting was a very good second. The sport of killing rats will be further dealt with in Section II, Sub-section I, under the head of " Ratting." Here I am chiefly concerned with their destruction by dogs, whether assisted by ferrets or not.

Rats are noxious vermin and the only consideration they deserve is that when they are killed they shall be killed quickly : the sooner the better, in fact.

The principal thing in killing rats with dogs is that sticks shall not also be employed in the slaughter. If they are, sooner or later some of the dogs will be injured irretrievably, very likely blinded, or even killed ; and a true sportsman would rather that a hundred rats should escape than that one dog should be hit with a stick in the hands of its excited wielder, even if the dog should not be seriously hurt. I have heard of cases in which the poor ferret has been so killed ; but that is absolutely inexcusable. The man who cannot distinguish between even a fitchy ferret and a rat ought to be thrust head foremost into a rat-riddled rick with his hands tied behind him and made to learn the difference. For killing rats the choice must be made between ferrets and sticks, or dogs and no sticks. It is the latter that I have here termed " rat-hunting," as distinguished from the former, which I have called " ratting."

Rats, unfortunately for the community and

fortunately for the sportsman, are to be found nearly everywhere : the difficulty being to get at the brutes.

The finest form of rat-hunting is, perhaps, seen when ferrets are introduced into a well-tenanted rick in the open fields, the rick being surrounded by sportsmen and dogs, the latter of whom nip up rat after rat as quickly as the ferrets bolt them. As many as 800 rats have been killed in this way in two days' sport on a Wiltshire Farm, by the terriers belonging to a well-known hunting-man in the New Forest.

The hunting of rats when thrashing is going on is a very second-rate form of the sport, as there are long waits between the bolting vermin, who generally collect in the bottom of the stack, and wait until the end, when they rush forth in a crowd, and many escape because the dogs are too few to cope with them. In a rickyard, too, there is often little space, and the rodents find it easy to take refuge in adjacent stacks or straw heaps, and under the sacks of grain, or the floors of barns and outbuildings.

Where rats haunt pig-sties it is a good plan to steal down at dusk with a terrier in the arms and pop it quietly and suddenly over the wall. There is usually some good if momentary sport ; though the dog will probably want a bath in strong Condy's Fluid and water if it is to sleep in the house afterwards.

In the early autumn banks and hedgerows may be ferreted for rats, there being at least one dog on either side of the hedge : of course well-broken to ferrets.

It is possible also to bait up a cellar for rats during a week or two, and then having on the eve of the selected night stopped up all doors and windows save one, enter suddenly by this with the dogs, who will have great fun by the light of an electric torch until all the rats have been killed.   It is as well not to wear trousers or slacks for this sport, as rats are sure to take refuge in them and not unlikely to nip their wearers. If they are worn, a pair of cycling clips should be placed round the ankles.

For entering young terriers, rats caught in box-traps may be used, being turned down in some small enclosed space from whence there is no chance of their escape.   If a good dog once gets a severe bite from a rat it will rouse its animosity against the vermin for life, and thereafter it will never miss a chance of killing them in a manner that will ensure the dog immunity from further punishment,

4. SQUIRREL-HUNTING

Although a picturesque little beast the squirrel is very destructive, and where very numerous it is a necessity to destroy it in order to avoid damage to plantations. Many thousands of squirrels are thus killed annually in Sutherlandshire and other counties where forestry is carried out on scientific lines, as is now likely to be the case throughout all parts of the United Kingdom.

Squirrels are partial hibernants and the season for hunting them is from spring to autumn. Terriers are used for the purpose in Highland Scotland. They hit off the drag of the squirrel and carry it to the tree it has last ascended from the ground, and in which it may be crouching concealed from human vision. A few smart taps with a stick will soon cause it to bolt, when it may ascend to a considerable height before taking a flying leap to an adjacent tree. This being marked, the tapping process is repeated, until the quarry is driven, perhaps, to the end of an avenue or the outskirts of a wood : when he must come to the ground and the terrier will get him. Even in large coverts squirrels get tired of jumping from tree to tree much more quickly than might be supposed, and sooner or later

descend to earth in the hope of finding cover in
bushes and undergrowth.   In " drawing " for a
squirrel many trees at which the terrier has marked
will be found " blank " ; but in such cases a cast
round the neighbouring trees in a circle will
usually end in discovering the one to which the
quarry has removed.   Where squirrels are at
all abundant hunting them is quite an exciting
sport, and a bag of a dozen or so should easily
be made in the course of an afternoon's sport.
Squirrels are excellent food for tame hawks and
in Brittany are made into pies.

5.   WATER-VOLE AND MOOR-HEN HUNTING

I have bracketed these two species of quarry
together because they live in the same streams,
and where one is found there will, in most instances,
be found the other also.   There must be few
streams upon which our little brown friend the
water-vole, commonly but wrongly called the
" water-rat," is not found ;   and the same may
be said of his feathered companion the moor-hen,
also known as the water-hen, which, in addition,
frequents the smallest field-ponds, provided there
be any sufficient cover in their vicinity.   Now,
although it is probably true that few, if any, living
creatures, were their life-history completely known,

would not be found to do more good than harm during their periods of existence—human beings alone excepted—it must always be the case that wherever from any cause they become too numerous, damage and loss to human interests results. Moor-hens eat an enormous quantity of growing grass, and water-voles honeycomb the banks of rivers and streams with holes, which in time of flood or from the wash of passing boats fill with water; and this, rushing back into the current, gradually disintegrates the banks, which crumble and fall into the stream. It is, therefore, almost necessary to thin out the numbers of both these creatures, and the most sporting way to do so is by hunting them with a keen dog that will take the water freely. Almost any terrier, or a cross-bred spaniel-terrier will do this, but it requires some patience to train them to kill their quarry successfully.

This sort of hunting is essentially an evening sport, and should be confined to warm weather, if the danger of rheumatism to the dogs employed is to be avoided; and in any case on the return home the dog should be rubbed thoroughly dry with a rough towel reserved for the purpose, unless it sleeps out of doors, when, given plenty of clean dry oaten or wheat straw, the dog will dry himself very quickly. Barley straw must never be used for any animal, as it breeds lice.

It takes a clever as well as a good dog to kill water-voles. They never feed far from their holes, and " plop " over the bank and into their homes very quickly. Whatever an Englishman's home may be, a water-vole's is certainly its castle ; and it won't permit any other water-vole to enter it, even to save its life. If you can hustle it so that it is forced away from it, its fate is generally settled, if the water is of suitable size and there is not too much flotsam about to afford it cover. One of my terriers owing to this habit once got two voles at a snap, having swum to a hole just as his quarry scrambled in, and while he was " winding " it the owner drove the intruder out again with such ferocity that they both fell into the dog's jaws.

In order to train a dog to kill water-voles, take him along the side of a small gently-moving brook when the shadows are lengthening. Don't have any human companions and only the one dog ; and don't whistle or call to him, for the sound of the human voice is fatal to sport. The voles will be nibbling herbage close to the edge, or may be climbing about just under the bank. When they feel the vibration of a footfall or

see the dog they will dive and go straight for
their holes. If these should be upon the opposite
bank a good " view " can be obtained and the
terrier will go in after them. If close enough
to scare the vole from its proper hole it will make
off up or down stream, travelling close to the
bottom and endeavouring, by stirring this up,
to conceal its movements under a cloud of mud.
It is not always easy to decide at once which way
a vole is travelling, as the current bears the
mud-cloud down with it, of course, though the
quarry may be going up-stream. This will baffle
the dog, and at first he will probably be uni-
formly unsuccessful, as he will generally swim
about waiting for the " rat " to show itself on the
surface, and have no idea of diving after it. However, when his futile excitement begins to cool,
pick him up in your arms and walk cautiously
on. Presently there will be another " plop,"
indicating that another water-vole has taken to
the stream. Now run quickly along the bank
till you can show the dog the vole travelling along
the bottom. Put him sharply down on the edge
opposite the moving beastie and he will probably
dive straight to the bottom and come up with the
quarry in his mouth. Once he does this he is

" entered," and will rarely miss his prey in future. It is the diving that does it.

Moor-hen hunting is somewhat different in its method of procedure. The call of the moor-hen will probably give the first clue to its where-abouts, or it may be seen flirting its white tail in and out of the reeds. Although it dives instan-taneously to the flash of a gun, it is slower to do so at sight of man or dog : I have even known a clever dog to swim quietly and rapidly after one and seize it before it could dive. When it dives the dog must swim about waiting for it to re-appear, which it generally does pretty soon. If it doesn't reappear after about a minute, it is certain to be hiding under the bank, and if a careful search be made it is often possible to put one's arm down and pull it out alive. Aware only of the pursuit of the dog it seems to ignore the dog's master on the bank. For this reason, where the water is too big to wade, it is useful to have a companion and perhaps another dog to work the opposite bank. Moor-hens seem to lose heart very easily when hunted in this way. I remember one winter hunting one on a small artificial leat with a spaniel who flushed the bird thrice, when it dived and entirely disappeared in clear water not two feet deep. After five minutes' search I saw its tail eighteen inches below the surface among some submerged weed under the bank. Baring my arm I took it out quite drowned and dead, its beak full of the weed it had clung to rather than face the chase again. A deliberate case of suicide?

Moor-hens do not fly far when flushed, and generally keep to the stream : so that they can be put up again and again, or if missed on the way up-stream can be re-found on the return journey. Sometimes, in summer, before the mowing-grass is cut, they will fly into it for refuge. A good dog, however, will mark the spot where the bird drops, go straight to the place and return with it in its mouth. Moor-hens are excellent eating, roasted and served with bread-sauce ; but they should be skinned, not plucked, and soaked for an hour or so in salt and water before cooking.

A word of caution about getting a young dog to take to the water. Never throw him into it : if he is reluctant to go, wade in yourself and encourage the dog to follow you. If he won't, put a lead on and take him through quietly at a place where he can feel his feet first and where there is no current, afterwards wading a bit deeper and obliging him to swim. Choose a day when the temperature of the water is high—best tested with

C

the calves of your own legs—and encourage and
make much of him directly he begins to show
signs of losing his reluctance. If you ever have
to *throw* a dog into water because it won't go
of its own accord, tie a weight round its neck at
the same time and have done with it once and
for ever !

6. WILD RABBIT-COURSING

This is where the whippet or the cross between
whippet and terrier comes in, and a very pretty
sport it is in suitable country, where permission
has been previously obtained. It is necessary
to find the rabbits lying out at some distance
from their burrows : either in the miniature
" formes " they make in tussocks of grass, dried
fern, or in other easily disturbed cover in open
meadows. Warm sunny days in autumn and
winter are, perhaps, the best for this very genuine
sport, but many buck-rabbits are found lying
out during the summer. The feeding hours of
rabbits are pretty well fixed as at early dawn,
again at about 11 o'clock, between 3 and
4 o'clock, and lastly about 6-30. The English
Home Office having omitted to notify British
rabbits of the ridiculous and unnatural
Summer-time regulations, they still continue to

observe times as regulated since the Creation by the sun. The sportsman must, therefore, make allowance for the wisdom of the rabbit in arranging his programme of sport. It is of little use coursing rabbits during their feeding hours, as they are then so numerous that the dogs get bewildered and confused, and soon lose their keenness, even if they don't get disheartened altogether.

The coursing dog should be trained to walk alongside his master, who with a stick will poke—not beat—likely tussocks and bunches of withered bracken until he starts the game, when the dog should jump into his stride and if the burrow be not too near overtake and kill his rabbit smartly. Once his turn of speed has been ascertained a slip-collar may be used, and according to the openness of the ground and the proximity of cover, a certain amount of " law " allowed. A slip-collar must be used for dogs that cannot be restrained without it from ranging ahead or trying to find the game themselves.

If the young sportsman can persuade one or more of his neighbours also to keep a whippet or whippet-terrier, he can get a pair of slips and they can enter into friendly competition with each other, each taking it in turn to slip the dogs when a rabbit is put up. Where there are several owners and dogs in the same neighbourhood miniature " coursing meetings " can be arranged, the dogs being drawn against each other, as at the Waterloo Cup Meeting, and run in ties or heats, so that the winner of the first tie comes in the next round against the winner of the second tie, and so on. In order to avoid the necessity of a judge the dog that kills the rabbit should be adjudged the winner ; not, as in greyhound coursing, the dog that scores most points towards a kill. Where the game escapes, it should be given as a " no course "; and where both dogs seize the rabbit together, as an " undecided " ; the heat in either case being run again.

I shall have more to say about whippets in Sub-section 8, under " Dog-racing." I will merely add that the whippet inherits from its Italian ancestors a certain sensitiveness to cold, and that when taken out in raw, damp weather, and having to be kept standing about waiting its turn to be put in slips, it should be protected by a coat, or sheet, which a mother, sister, or sewing-maid can easily make : though, of course, they are to be bought from saddlers in districts where whippet-racing is a favourite pursuit of the local miners and artizans. Naturally when more than two dogs are taken out the non-competing animals must be securely led, to prevent their breaking away and spoiling a trial.

7. HEDGEHOG-FINDING

Although it takes a good dog to kill a hedgehog, most dogs with a nose are capable of finding them. In fact, hedgehogs are a fascinating puzzle to dogs and appear to carry a strong scent, since even a spaniel when out with the gun can seldom be prevailed upon to pass one, although it be rolled in dead leaves under thick undergrowth during its hibernating period.

It usually takes a dog some time to learn that the hedgehog has a vulnerable spot, though foxes and badgers have no difficulty in the matter ; but when he does find out the secret the hedgehog has a very poor chance despite his sharp bristles.

The best time of year to look for hedgehogs is in the early autumn when their family cares are over and they have fattened themselves up for their winter sleep. The places in which they are to be found are rather numerous, but as their name implies, the hedgerows, especially those surrounding game-coverts, are the most likely,

provided they are bounded by deep ditches full
of dead leaves : in fact " ditch-hog " would be a
better name for this small insectivorous and
egg-sucking animal than " hedgehog." Even
in the coverts themselves the beast prefers a pit
or a dyke to a more elevated position.

Hedgehogs, as most people know by this time,
are very good eating : a delicacy, in fact, and
should only be killed when required for food.
If the sportsman's dog cannot kill them, they
must be taken home in a sack or game-bag—
lay this on the ground and roll the hedgehog
into it with the foot—and then placed face downwards into a tub containing two or three inches
of water. Rather than drown, the animal will
presently put out his head, when a smart
tap on the snout with a hammer will do its
business.

Hedgehogs, however, are very interesting
pets and most useful in a house, especially in
a town house, which they will keep completely
free from cockroaches and other insects ; and
in a walled garden they are invaluable. If the
garden is not walled, however, they will soon
wander away into the open country.

During the war, when butcher's meat was
severely rationed, I went in for hedgehogs rather

extensively, and with the aid of a spaniel called
" Dash," found so many that, had they been
killed, the larder would have been overstocked. So
I had to keep them alive. One was rather unenter-
prizing, and, after a ramble round the garden,
returned through the coal-hatch and then retired
under a fixed dresser in a basement kitchen and
was seen no more until the following spring.

The other I turned down in the kitchen in the
presence of an interested kitten. After a short
time it uncurled and became inquisitive, and on
pouring some milk on the linoleum in front of it,
it speedily began to lap it up, much to the disgust
of the cat. In two days it was quite tame and
would allow its head to be stroked gently without
withdrawing it, looking slyly out of one eye at
the stroker. It selected as a sleeping-place a
corner in which the brooms and brushes were
kept, but never attempted to hibernate. Indeed
it soon became very enterprising, and would
walk upstairs in the early morning, enter my
bedroom, and having found a piece of Indian
matting surrounding a dressing-table, would go
round and round it at an incredible rate of speed
and refuse to stop until absolutely turned out
of the room. It seemed to like the sound of its
own feet pattering on a hard shiny surface, so

different from anything it had known in the woods and fields, and it came upstairs like a steam-engine. The first time was rather disastrous, as it met the housekeeper coming downstairs with a tray in her hands, and as she promptly sat down and let go the tray in order to hold her skirts around her legs, besides screaming loudly, the hedgehog must have thought that the end of all possible worlds had come. However, they became quite friendly in the long run, and she even assisted at a surgical operation on " Hotchy." It was noticed going lame one day, and I found that two of the front toes of one foot were tightly bound together with some foreign substance. A magnifying glass showed this to be human hair, which it had probably been scraping out of the brooms and brushes used for sweeping the bedroom floors. I held " Hotchy " up by the two fore-legs, its little head leaning sideways on my hand, and its quick eye watching everything keenly while the hairs were snipped and unravelled. There must have been at least a foot of hair binding the toes together. Being replaced on the floor it at once started on a " joy-race " up and down the passage, exhibiting evident signs of relief. It could beat the cat easily in a race of 20 yards or so, going at a swift trot; while she progressed by leaps and bounds.

One thing to be guarded against by the boy who keeps hedgehogs as pets is the danger of their getting roasted alive. Roast hedgehog is a delicacy, but the animal must be correctly treated before being cooked. A hedgehog will climb into any oven the door of which is left open—I have known a cat do the same—and I once found " Hotchy " at midnight rolled up in the warm ashes in the ash-pan under the kitchen grate, though the fire above was not out and there were plenty of red-hot cinders that might have fallen on him.

Hedgehog-finding can, you see, be made (in addition to being a sport in itself) useful and interesting in its results ; whether from a culinary point of view or from that of the student of natural history and the habits of wild animals in semi-captivity.

8. DOG-RACING

This is a distinct sport from coursing rabbits, although dogs of the same breed, whippets or whippet-terriers, or even terriers proper, may be employed. It is, in fact, recognised as among the second-rate Major Sports of Great Britain;

there having been, prior to the War, a very large
number of organized public dog-racing grounds
both in Scotland and England, which in process
of time will probably be reopened—under new
or old management.

Every boy who owns a dog knows how easily
it can be induced to race to its master if held
by someone else while that master retires to a
suitable distance ; and especially if the master
waves a white or coloured " rag " to attract its
attention. The whole secret of dog-racing,whether
privately pursued in a paddock adjoining one's
home, or on an open common, or in a large
regularly-organized racing enclosure, lies in
this teaching of a dog to race to a " rag."

First, it is encouraged to hang on to and worry
the piece of stuff, dignified with this technical
name, at all odd moments : then it is held by the
collar while its master or someone else, waving
the rag, runs backwards for a certain number
of yards in full view of the dog, which when
released races hot-foot to regain possession of
the rag.

Of course competition between the dogs of
various owners is the essence of this sport ; and
during the summer months a very pretty and
pleasant pastime it is in country districts, where

time hangs heavily, or at least seems to pass
slowly. There is no necessity for the elaborate
machinery of the professional Dog-Racing
Grounds : the starting pistol, the sunken judge's
box, the low boards dividing the cinder or brick-
dust course lengthwise, the coloured collars and
telegraph-board, nor for the use of the dog-racing
" Handicapper's Tables " with their elaborate
system of handicapping by weight and previous
performances. All that is required is a fairly
level piece of greensward, about 250 yards long,
a pole for winning post, with a tape stretched
thence to the waterproof-sheet on which the
judge lies prone, so as to bring his eyes on a
level with the competitors; another pole for
" overmark " fifty yards farther on, and a
sufficient number of youths and boys to hold
the dogs at the starting point while their owners
run backwards up the course, waving their rags
to encourage their dogs to race. The signal
to despatch the little competitors must not be
given before the " runners-up " have passed the
winning-post, and they should all have passed
the " overmark " before the first dog breasts the
tape held in the judge's hand.

Any sufficiently fast dog is eligible for this
sort of racing ; while a rough system of

handicapping up to 30 or 40 yards out of 200 may be founded on the principle of putting a pure-bred whippet at scratch, and dogs that, by reason of the shortness of their legs or bulk of their bodies, look less likely to possess any turn of speed at various distances in advance : the signal to start being given by a short, sharp whistle, as the dropping of a flag or a handkerchief would be likely to distract the attention of the nearest competitors.

A small sweepstakes or pool consisting of entrance fees, to go to the winner, may add attraction to this form of sport ; or perhaps a wealthy uncle may be " tapped " to provide a useful prize for the winning dog or dogs.

The summer months in the cool of the evening are perhaps best for dog-racing of this sort ; although, of course, there is no reason why it should not be pursued in favourable weather at almost any season of the year : and the same animal may be used for coursing rabbits when that sport becomes practicable.

9. Hunting " the Clean Boot "

This is the sport of the bloodhound-breeder, but practically all dogs that hunt by scent— that is, every kind of dog except the greyhound and the whippet—can be taught to hunt "the clean boot," which means an ordinary article of footwear not rubbed with aniseed or any other scent. The bloodhound is popularly supposed to refuse to hunt his own master; but other dogs are not so particular, and would, in fact, prefer to hunt their masters rather than strangers.

Most dogs will hunt or follow their masters by scent in any case; but the method of training them to hunt other people is very simple. In the first place the dog must be held by the collar while the person who is to act as " runner " pats him on the head and thus attracts his attention.

He should then start off at a run (calling the dog, which is still firmly held), and maintain the pace until he is out of sight, when he may drop into a walk for the remainder of the distance. At first this should be short and the course fairly straight, say 300 or 400 yards, and should end at a tree or bush behind which the ' runner " can conceal himself. The holder of the dog, directly he judges the runner to have reached the allotted spot and before the dog's attention has been distracted from the fact that the man who petted and called him has disappeared at a run, should release the straining dog, who should get its nose down at once and follow at top-speed. If it is keen it will keep its nose down until it actually runs bang against the human quarry, when it will dance about with joy, bark with pleasure, and should be promptly rewarded by the runner himself with a small piece of raw meat or a lump of sugar, as the case may be.

Once an intelligent terrier understands that the finding of the person who disappears suddenly at a run is what is expected of it, it is astonishing how quickly it enters into the fun of the thing, and how keen it becomes to follow the scent.

The distance, and consequently the amount of " law " allowed, will be gradually extended until a run of a mile or even two miles may be enjoyed. For the benefit of stationary spectators this may be made in the shape of a horse-shoe or circle, care being taken that the runner never comes into view of the dog before it is released after he first disappears from sight. It should always be the runner who should reward the dog on being " treed " or found, never the holder, whichever of the twain happens to be its owner.

The training of dogs to hunt the clean boot may occasionally be of considerable service, since if a person who has gone out for a walk in an unknown direction is suddenly wanted in a hurry the dog may be laid on his scent at the spot where the man was last seen and sent off on its quest, perhaps with a cord or note tied to its collar, and much valuable time saved in this way; provided, of course, that too long a time has not elapsed since he went out.

II : SPORTS DEPENDING CHIEFLY ON FERRETS

PRELIMINARY NOTES

FERRETS, although now rather dear to buy, are yet quite a good investment. Not only are they now, and likely to be, in some request both for rabbiting and ratting, but if the young sportsman will buy both a hob and a jill, provide them with proper living-accommodation and look after them as he should, he can easily make a reasonable amount of pocket-money by breeding and selling their offspring.

Ferrets are of two sorts, the light-coloured or albino variety with pink eyes, and the larger dark-eyed, partially light-coloured sort that exhibits a closer resemblance to their common ancestor, the polecat. The former runs smaller than the latter and can get into small rat-holes which the bigger " fitchy " ferret cannot enter ; but on the other hand the fitchy ferret is, as a rule, bolder in tackling an old buck rat in a corner, especially the jill.

If ferrets are to be kept they must have consistent attention or they will not repay keeping. There is probably no sporting pet that requires more. Not only must they be kept scrupulously clean, but they must be given fresh air, plenty of exercise—a matter too often neglected—and regular food, occasionally varied, and their domicile must be well-ordered on an invariable principle.

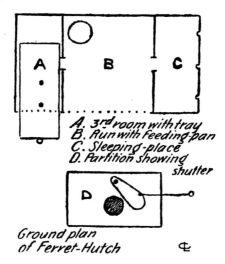

A. 3rd room with tray
B. Run with feeding-pan
C. Sleeping-place
D. Partition showing
                    shutter

Ground plan
of Ferret-Hutch

Various firms offer for sale well-designed ferret hutches; but it is simple enough, if the diagrams given in this book are followed, to make a good ferret-hutch out of a box bought from the grocer for a shilling or two. A ferret-court with a hutch set in its midst, is, of course, the best way to keep ferrets in perfect health, as they

D

can then get plenty of fresh air and exercise at will, and yet preserve a place of retreat in wet weather or when they wish to sleep or lie-up. Given a tiled yard it is not difficult to board off a portion as a court for ferrets. But the floor should be well covered with peat-moss litter or sawdust and the ferrets confined to their hutches on wet days.

The hutch itself must not stand on the ground and should be divided into three compartments, one for sleeping in, one to serve as a feeding-place, and the third as a resort for sanitary purposes. The sleeping-compartment should be at one end and the feeding-place and run (where there is no ferret-court) in the centre. A round hole should be cut in each of the partitions, as shown in the diagram, to give access to the different compartments ; and both holes should be provided with a shutter so as to confine the ferrets when necessary. There should be a few ventilation-holes cut in the outside ends of the first and third compartments. The roof should be covered with a piece of canvas or felt to render it waterproof, and should be hinged, and overlap in front and at the ends to run the rain off clear of the sides. This roof-lid should be made in three sections, the centre section being less than the full size of the compartment, which will allow of the others overlapping and so helping to maintain the sleeping compartment in a dry state. The floor of the sleeping compartment and run will be the bottom of the box ; but in the third compartment a zinc tray—the cover of a large square tin biscuit-box may be made to serve—must be fitted, which can be drawn out to be cleaned. If sawdust is kept in this it will be the easier to clean. The sleeping compartment must be filled with dry wood-shavings. Nothing should be put on the floor of the run, except the food dishes and flesh-food, when given. A little disinfectant may be dropped into the water used to wash out the removable floor of the third compartment and the wood-work if necessary ; and there may be a couple of holes punched in the zinc tray, corresponding with similar holes in the wooden floor of the box itself, for drainage purposes. The front of the box will be faced with small-meshed wire-netting or else with a grating of narrow bars : the former for preference. The front of the sleeping-box will be boarded up and the only light to penetrate into the interior will come through the three small ventilation-holes cut in the end under the eaves of the roof-lid. The hutches should be out-of-doors, elevated from the ground, and sheltered at the back by a wall.

The best food for ferrets is oatmeal porridge and milk, given regularly every morning except on working-days, when the meal will be given when the ferrets are brought home in the evening. The pan containing it should be taken away as soon as the ferrets have finished eating, and not left to become stale and sour. Twice a week a freshly-killed bird or rat or part of a rabbit, given while they are still warm, should be allowed them in addition to and after the oatmeal porridge. The shutter of the sleeping-room aperture should be closed when this is done, to prevent the ferrets dragging the flesh into this compartment and so soiling their bedding. Flesh meat should not be allowed to remain more than a quarter of an hour, just long enough for them to suck the blood out, and must then be removed. If oatmeal porridge is unobtainable, bread-and-milk makes a fair substitute.

If ferrets are treated in this way they should never have any disease, and if their feet are washed in Condy's Fluid and water after work they will never even have " foot-rot." Two hutches will be necessary if the young sportsman goes in for breeding, as the hob must not be kept with

the jill after they have paired. When the jill
has had her young they should not be disturbed,
nor even looked at, for at least a month, a fresh
bed being made up for the mother a week before
her litter is due. Her food should be put quietly
in every day at the same hour, and she should
then be left in peace. In any case it is advisable
to have two hutches, so that one may be in use
while the other is being disinfected.

If ferrets require muzzling for rabbits a string
muzzle should be used, tied first round the neck
with a small loop in the string to come on the
head between the ears, then again round the
mouth, with a knot under the chin and another
on the nose, the longer end of the string being
thence carried up to and through the loop and
brought back down the forehead to meet and be
fastened to the shorter end. This makes a simple
and efficient ferret muzzle ; but the less you have
tó muzzle a ferret or work it on a line the better.
Of course you can do neither when ratting.

I think a coat pocket with a little dry hay in it
the best place to carry a ferret. At any rate a bag
should never be used. If pockets are unavailable
a box with hay—and some ventilation holes—
should be used, as this, like a flapped pocket,
will keep the ferret warm and dry in any weather.

Remember that the more fresh air and exercise they get the healthier and better workers they will be. If they are not kept in a ferret-court they should be turned out on the tennis-lawn or some enclosed place for half an hour every fine day, and allowed to gallop about and stretch their limbs at will.

To pick up a ferret safely, put your thumb and fore-finger round its neck from above and behind, and get its off fore-paw between your first and second fingers. So held it cannot possibly bite the holder, and can be lifted and carried with comfort to itself.

1. RATTING

Ferreting rats is grand sport, whether out of ricks and hedgerows, or the drains, walls, and floors of old houses, barns, and stables ; but it must be definitely decided beforehand whether, when the rats bolt, they are to be killed by blows from sticks or by terriers only. As I have said before, dogs and sticks must never be employed together.

In ferreting a corn-stack the holes along the bottom of the stack should be stopped, and the ferrets placed on the roof to find their way downwards to the basement, driving the bulk of the rats before them. Some will come out under the eaves, of course, and take flying leaps into the mouths of the dogs, or offer the chances of swiping blows with the sticks, as the case may be. But when these fugitives from the upper stories have ceased to emerge and the ferrets begin to show out again, it is time to unstop the holes round the bottom of the stack and put the ferrets in there—when the fun, if there are plenty of rats in the stack, will become fast and furious.

Ferreting stables, outbuildings, and drains is a slower game altogether, especially in unknown or unfamiliar surroundings, as there is no saying where the ferrets may go or where to look for them should they chance to lie-up. Here I think dogs are preferable to sticks for killing the rats. Very often there is no space to wield a stick properly, and where there are so many bolt-holes it is impossible to guard them all, whereas a dog can very often overtake a rat that would get out of reach of the man with a stick.

Hedgerow-ratting is also good sport in the early autumn, before the rats have got into the stacks and outhouses; but here again ferrets lying-up often cause delay. Where there is only one ferret he must, of course, be dug out, a plan impracticable in the case of walls and drains; but if there is a good supply of ferrets, it is best to go on and leave a box with some hay in it where the ferret went in. It will, on emerging, creep unto the box and so be recaptured and carried home.

The ideal hedge for ferreting rats is one with a gateway in the middle, at which someone should be stationed with stick or dog to catch those rats that try to streak to safety across the aperture. The hedge should be ferreted up to the gateway from one end, and then a move should be made to the far end of the hedgerow and the process repeated back to the gateway. Sticks in the hands of skilled "marksmen" will do more execution than dogs in hedgerow-ferreting, as the latter are often beaten by the rats popping into other holes before the terriers can snap them up.

2. RABBITING

The principal adjunct to the ferret in rabbiting is a net, of which an illustration is provided below. Every sportsman ought to be able to make his own nets, although instructions for acquiring a knowledge of this handicraft do not fall within the province of this little book. In any case rabbit-nets can be bought for a few pence ready made.

The great secret of success in ferreting rabbits into nets lies in approaching the burrows in silence and working quietly. Otherwise the bunnies will refuse to bolt and simply lie kicking while the ferrets suck their blood if unmuzzled, or scratch at them with their claws if muzzled.

Rabbit-net

On approaching the selected burrow, examine it carefully and decide which is the main entrance: there is always a " front door," so to speak, to a rabbit-burrow. Having ascertained this, peg the nets strongly above each of the other exits or entrances. One or more strong pegs driven in above the hole should be sufficient to keep the net in its place and the bulk of the net should hang below the hole. When the nets have been so arranged, put the ferret into the front door without any net over it, of course, and then crouch down quietly where you cannot be seen by a bolting rabbit. Watch all the nets all the time, and the moment a rabbit jumps into one steal softly out, pick up the bunny, replace the net at once (as they very often follow each other out of the same hole in quick succession) and then kill the rabbit noiselessly and retreat out of sight as expeditiously and quietly as possible.

If you have a reliable, steady, and fast dog, one that won't bark, and will keep close to his master, he may be taken out, provided he is " broken to ferret," for the purpose of stopping any rabbit that may emerge from an un-netted hole ; but if he gives tongue in chase he will be worse than useless ; and in most cases of ferreting rabbits their capture in the nets should be relied upon as sufficient.

Ferrets that can only be worked upon a line are a nuisance ; but if you are far from home and a ferret lies up and has to be dug, a second ferret, lined, may be sent in after it, to locate the place, and when this has been done this second ferret is withdrawn and digging commences. Even so, care must be taken that there are no roots or

other obstacles on which the line can get hung
up. Otherwise the ferret must be left and the
box of hay placed at the mouth of the hole it
last entered, as described in the previous section.
Bells on ferrets are absolutely fatal to sport,
and since no one can hear them when the ferret
is underground, are also useless—unless, of course,
they are blind men's ferrets.

If a ferret is very wet and dirty after its day's
work it should be washed in lukewarm water and
Condy's Fluid and carefully dried before being
replaced in the hutch and fed. In any case its
feet must always be so treated after work. If
ferrets are properly fed at all times and allowed
to slake their thirst before being worked, and
if they are kept supplied with animal food, as
laid down in the Preliminary Notes, they should
very seldom lie-up. Very cold weather may
induce them to do so, but ferreting rabbits is not
an ideal occupation for youthful sportsmen in
very cold weather, and some more clement day
should be chosen in preference. Not, however,
when a high wind is blowing, for rabbits will not
bolt well on windy days—small blame to them.

III: SPORTS DEPENDENT ON BIRDS

1. HAWKING SMALL BIRDS

THE only hawk likely to be within reach of the youthful falconer is the sparrow-hawk : though in some parts of the country it is easier to get a cast of merlins from a nest found in the heather on some moorland hill in Scotland, Northern England, Wales, or Ireland.

Merlins are delightful little falcons, chiefly used for hawking larks ; though they are high-couraged enough to take pigeons, and even partridges. They are usually flown in pairs (called a " cast ") and require an open down country to display their qualities properly, which usually means a pony in order to follow and take them up. They belong to the family of true falcons, or long-winged hawks, like the peregrine. Unfortunately they are disappointing birds to possess, because they nearly always die during the first winter ; and for this and other reasons I do not propose to say any more about them.

The sparrow-hawk, which has become very common nearly everywhere during the last few years, belongs to the family of true hawks, or short-winged hawks like the goshawk, which

SPARROW-HAWK

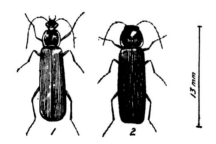

1. SOLDIER BEETLE.   2. SAILOR BEETLE.

[Face p. 60.

no longer breeds in the British Isles. The nest of the sparrow-hawk is not difficult to find, as more often than not it is a last year's deserted crow's, magpie's, or woodpigeon's nest. Birds intended to be trained for hawking must be taken from the nest, and that at precisely the right moment: which is on the day that they are fully fledged, having lost all their down, but have not actually flown: what, were they peregrine falcons, would be known as "eyas hawks," as opposed to the "passage hawks" or full-grown birds captured on migration. It follows, therefore, that when the nest from which the birds are to be taken has been discovered—a species of minor sport in itself—it must be carefully watched from day to day to ascertain the right moment for removing the young birds. The larger of these will prove to be females and the smaller males, or "muskets." There is also a considerable difference in plumage, the females being brown with a white breast barred with greyish-umber, while the musket is slate-grey, with a dull white breast barred with dark-brown and rufous, the tail brownish with dusky bars. This is the adult plumage; the young birds resemble the female bird, but leave a general impression of rufous colouring in the upper parts.

Once the nest has been found it will be well if the young sportsman makes friends with the keeper, if there be one, and persuades him not to follow his custom of firing a charge of shot into the nest, nor to kill the parent birds until the young have been secured. From four to six eggs are usually hatched, but two young birds will be enough to take. Choose those that have obviously " done themselves well," as their feathers will eventually prove stronger and have no signs of " hunger-trace " to cause them to break in later days. As the young falconer will probably only fly at small birds, blackbirds and thrushes chiefly, the musket will serve him as well as the female ; though the latter if a good one can take partridges easily. He may take one of each sex or two females and a male if he would like to have more, but should be warned that by so doing he is adding to his responsibilities, as the short-winged hawks require constant attention and care, and require to be carried on the fist for several hours daily as a part of their training. One hawk is really as much as the youthful sportsman can look after and train properly ; and one really well-trained hawk is worth more than two or three moderate ones.

Hawk's Jess

In order to keep sparrow-hawks, a " mews " should be provided. This may be a quite small outhouse such as a woodshed, with a doorway fitted with a frame covered with wire-netting. The original door should be retained, however, as it will be necessary to close it in order to darken the mews. At first the young birds may be placed in a square hamper nailed to the wall, with the lid extended and supported so as to form a ledge. Here they must be fed by candle-light (in the darkened outhouse) for the first day or two, the raw meat they are given being placed on the falconer's wrist and the bird encouraged to take it thence. It should never be allowed to have any food that it will not take from the hand ; and nothing should be done that is calculated to startle it in any way, for the sparrow-hawk is a very nervous little hawk and requires to be treated with the utmost gentleness and care.

When the birds are able to leave the hamper for good, a screen-perch (see illustration) must be provided. This is simply a pole about two inches in diameter with the bark left on, with a piece of canvas tacked on its under-side, and hanging down to the ground for a distance of about three feet. The hawk will be fastened to this, as explained later, and the screen will compel it to come up on the same side as it went down, should it flutter to the ground, and thus prevent the jesses and leash from getting entangled and twisted round the pole.

Screen-Perch
& Bow-Perch

For out-of-doors a bow perch will be required, instead of the block used for the long-winged hawks. An old perambulator—or bicycle—or other small wheel makes the best, and is simply stuck in the ground almost up to its axle ; the upper half-segment, unless possessing a solid rubber tyre, must be padded with tow and covered with coarse canvas to provide comfortable foothold. A bath about six inches deep should be provided every day, placed out-of-doors within reach of the bow-perch, when the hawk is being " weathered."

The young hawks should be fed three times a day to begin with, and afterwards twice : sparingly in the morning if to be flown, with a full meal in the evening. The food should consist of strips of tender beef, or rabbit's flesh, with that of small birds, or pigeons or even squirrels if they can be given freshly-killed and still warm, as a change of diet. Once a week the hawk should have a " gorge" or full meal, as much as ever he likes to eat ; and, on at least three days in each week, " castings " must be given. A " casting " is a piece of the skin of a bird or beast with the feathers or fur adhering : the skin of the head and neck of a fowl or pigeon or of a rabbit or squirrel makes a good casting. It should be big enough to make four or five good mouthfuls for the hawk. The casting is returned by the bird on the following morning in the shape of a pellet ; and it is by examining these pellets that the falconer may ascertain the condition and state of health of his charge. The pellet should be quite sweet to the smell, and hard, dry, and firm ; if it be otherwise the hawk is out of condition.

E

The training of a sparrow-hawk is in itself
simple, save that it requires the greatest patience
and care. It consists in so taming it that it
will feed without reluctance on the hand ; and
it must never otherwise be fed. The next step
is to get it to jump from the perch to the hand
for food. And the third to come to the fist
from as far off as the bird can see the falconer.
In short, the hawk must learn to regard the
falconer's fist as home, otherwise it will take
to trees when out and refuse to be called down.
It is from the fist that the bird will be flown at
the quarry, and to the fist that he will return
after a successful or unsuccessful flight.

Since sparrow-hawks are not flown at hack like
peregrine falcons they do not require bells ;
and unless they have to travel, they do not require
hoods either. They do, however, like other hawks,
need jesses, which should be placed upon their
legs directly they are taken from the nest and
never again removed. When the bird is sitting
on the fist, which should be protected by a
stout leather driving-glove or gauntlet-glove,
the jesses will be held through the fingers like
reins. When the hawk is to be attached to its
perch, a leash is required fitted with a double
swivel, to which one of the jesses is fastened,

the other end of the leash being attached to the perch.

The illustration shows what a jess is. They must be made of soft leather—dogskin or what is called " kip " (a kind of calf-leather) is best— and should be greased with vaseline or saddle-soap from time to time in order to prevent them from getting hard and stiff, through exposure to water when the hawk is bathing. Any boy should be able to cut out a pair of jesses by the aid of the accompanying pattern, which is drawn to a scale ($\frac{1}{4}$ inch=1 inch) to show its size and the position of the slits.

The larger end with the two slits is placed round the hawk's leg, and the point put through the slit nearer the middle of the jess. Then the narrow end is brought up and passed through both slits, the middle one first, and pulled taut. The leash should be of the same kind of leather, a yard in length, having a Turk's-head knot at one end to stop it from running through the swivel-ring. The latter must be a double one, and is fastened to the jess by passing the latter through one ring of the swivel and then passing both rings through the slit in the end of the hanging-part of the jess.

Since sparrow-hawks are " hawks of the fist,"

no lure is required for their training as is the case
with the falcons or " hawks of the lure," so
that the accessories for these birds are seen to be
few, simple, and inexpensive.

When a bird is trained it should be put out
each morning on the bow-perch, attached thereto
by the leash, in a corner of the tennis-lawn or
other quiet spot on turf, the bath placed within.
reach, and the bird left for two hours to " weather."
At the end of that time the young falconer
should call the hawk to his fist and feed it ; and
for the rest of the day until after the evening
meal, when it is returned to the screen-perch in
the mews or outhouse, it should be off the fist
as little as possible, and should accompany its
proud owner everywhere.

The method of hawking with these birds is
also simple. Blackbirds and thrushes are the
chief quarry, of course, and one or two bagged
ones—those caught under the fruit nets in the
garden will do—must be used to enter the bird.
Take the hawk into the middle of a large field,
where no hedge is within reach of the blackbird,
and get a companion to release the latter a few
yards in front of you on receiving the signal.
Release the jesses from your fingers, raising
the left hand with the bird sharply upwards

and forwards to the height of your head, and the hawk will leave the fist and go straight for the bird. If it strikes, brings down and binds to the quarry, it will allow itself to be taken up on the fist ; and, if it misses through the blackbird " putting-in " to a hedge, the hawk should return to the fist again at once.

The best place in which to find blackbirds and thrushes is an open field of roots in the early autumn ; and a spaniel or other dog, well under control, is useful to flush the birds. Another plan is to beat the hedgerows, which requires a companion on the opposite side of the hedge to put the birds out to the falconer, who will stand back and at a little distance from the hedge, so as to give the quarry a chance of flying away without " putting-in " again, as it too often does.

Falconry is one of the finest and oldest sports in the world ; and I think I have shown that it is within the scope of the minor sportsman, provided he be the right sort of boy and will take pains and exercise patience with his hawk. These are two qualities that will make for his success in after life, and he cannot practice them more pleasantly than in training a " hawk of the fist." Therefore, were I a parent I should never object to his carrying his hawk even in the house ;

or were I a schoolmaster, to his bringing it
into the class-room.   And this is a word to
persons who are not always so " sapient," as
they would have the youthful sportsman to
believe.

2. Trapping and Netting Sparrows

The house-sparrow is in most places as much
vermin as is the rat, and merits extinction—were
that possible—in the same degree.   It is, however,
so " 'cute " a bird that it becomes a true sport
to pit one's intellect against it, since it is considerably more than 3 to 1 that the sparrow comes off
best in the contest.

There are two more or less wholesale ways
of catching sparrows : first the clap-net method,
and second the screen or sieve trap.

As the illustration shows, the clap-net consists
of two 10 or 12-foot poles to which the net is
fastened like a Trades Union processionist's
banner ; but the bottom of the net is turned up
for two or three feet, thus forming a bag into
which the netted sparrows should—they don't
always—flutter down and become entangled.
It takes three sportsmen to net sparrows : two
to manage the net—and they will have to learn
to work in unison—and a third to hold a bright
light in a lanthorn, or a powerful electric torch
in the proper place.

Sparrow-trap

The happy hunting-grounds for sparrow-netting are ricks, and ivy-covered frontages of buildings to which, when the cold weather draws on in late autumn and during the winter months, the sparrows resort for roosting purposes. It is well to plan a sparrow-netting expedition with a little care and thought, so as first to visit places from which the escaped sparrows will fly to a sort of final refuge, where the last trial of the evening will be made, and with luck the biggest bag secured.

The *modus operandi* is for the sportsmen to approach the ivy-covered wall silently after dark on a dry, moonless night, and about two hours after the birds have gone to roost. The pole-bearers should stand close up to the wall with the poles sloped over their shoulders. Then at a preconcerted signal they should clap the poles simultaneously close against the ivy and hold them there, the bag part of the net being, of course, inside, against the lower part of the ivy. At the same signal their companion with the lanthorn or torch, hitherto obscured, should flash his light, from a little distance, full on the centre of the extended net. The startled birds will at once fly out towards the light, and finding themselves held back by the net will flutter and struggle downwards until they are caught in the bag below.

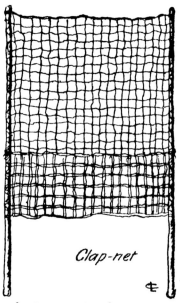

Clap-net

Don't be in too great a hurry to remove the net, and when you first do so bring the poles together in an upright position, still keeping them close to the wall, and when they meet reverse them smartly and lay the whole apparatus on the ground, when the captured birds can be removed one by one and placed in a basket carried by the lanthorn-bearer or by a fourth participant in the sport.

The first catch secured in this way, the net is again unfurled and a move made to the next " covert." Ivy-covered walls will be found more productive " draws " than ricks, as it is easier for the birds that roost under the eaves of the latter to escape over the top of the net, while many of them are so far back in the holes under the thatch that they won't " bolt " at all.

For trapping sparrows hard weather is necessary, and a clear space somewhere in the vicinity of the outhouse which is to serve as a place of concealment for the man who pulls the string. The screen or sieve must be set in position and allowed to remain there untouched for several days before it is sought to operate, as it will take all that time for the suspicious sparrows to get used to its appearance. Food must be regularly scattered there—and nowhere else in the vicinity —two or three times a day, until the birds have quite become accustomed to feeding there in security. Otherwise the machinery is quite simple, consisting only of a stick supporting the screen or sieve and about fifty feet of string fastened

to the stick and led to a hole in the door of the
outhouse. This door should be further provided
with a peep-hole through which the sportsman
can observe the ground under the trap. An
extra appetizing meal having been provided,
preferably by an accomplice who will at once
retire—the operator of the string having gone
into concealment some time previously—the
latter will watch and wait until a goodly number
of sparrows has congregated at the banquet,
and then give the string a smart jerk, when the
screen falling will cover a certain proportion of
the feeding birds.

There is some use in this sport, as sparrow-pie
is by no means to be despised if a little bacon
and plenty of pepper be used ; while, if only a
few birds are caught, they can be roasted before
the schoolroom fire and if basted with fat and well
peppered, make an appetizing " extra " to the
schoolroom tea. In addition to this, freshly-
killed sparrow is good for both ferrets and hawks.

I have said nothing here or elsewhere in this
book about the setting of gins, snares or spring-
traps, or the use of bird-lime. All these methods
of taking game are inhumane and unsportsmanlike,
and I hope none of my readers will ever employ
them. They should be left to poachers and those

professional rabbit-catchers who have to make a living by supplying the dealers and markets.

3. PIGEON-RACING

This is pre-eminently a sport in which the country boy who is fond of bird-pets can take an active and useful part, and one that will train him on to become perhaps in time a regular member of the homing-pigeon racing fraternity.

In the meantime the winning of 500-mile championships, or 50-guinea cups does not come into his scheme : if he be wise, a bird that will beat his next-door neighbour's bird or take home a message that he won't be in to tea will satisfy all his ambitions.

There are only two safe ways of acquiring racing pigeons. You can either buy a pair of old birds and breed from them, in which case they must be kept permanently in captivity ; or you can buy " squeakers " or " squabs." It is of little use buying young birds that have been fledged long enough to fly, unless you know their breeders, and know them also to be trustworthy persons. It is a sad fact, but true, that among professional breeders of racing pigeons there are nearly as many rogues as honest men, and a greater proportion of rogues *per centum* than in any other sport or profession—association-football and money-lending not excepted. Nearly all the fully-fledged young birds that the tyro is likely to have a chance of purchasing from unknown dealers have already been flown from their lofts, and once the money for them has been received, and they are allowed to fly from their new homes, are likely to return to the breeders : when the tyro may bid them adieu, as before he can go and identify them they will have been sold to someone else with a similar object in view.

It may be laid down as an axiom that any homing pigeon, which—given a fair chance according to age, distance, and weather-conditions—fails to return to its own loft after release, is not worth its food ; and it is upon this principle that the breeders of racing youngsters for sale to the uninitiated chiefly act.

Unless, therefore, the youthful sportsman is prepared to buy a pair of matched birds, and to provide a " prison " for them in which they may being up their young, and to wait until these are full-grown before beginning to indulge in the sport of pigeon-racing, he will be well-advised to buy " squeakers."

Squeakers are young pigeons in the nest,

A Flying Tippler.
(*By kind permission of " Pigeons and the Pigeon World "*)

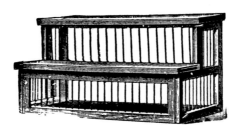

Trap for Racing-Pigeons.

[*Face p.* 76.

just on the point of being full-fledged, and can
be bought for much less than the delusive " young
bird that has never been outside the loft " of
the advertizing pigeon-merchant. If bought as
squeakers unable to fly, there can be no doubt
that, whatever their ultimate value as racers,
they will not go back to swell the ill-gotten gains
of their breeders. Also, since their merits are
untried and unknown they ought to be cheap :
though this, of course, will depend on the pedigree
and performances of their parents. My
recommendation to the youthful. sportsman,
therefore, is to commence by purchasing half
a dozen squeakers from the nearest reputable
breeder he can find.

There can be no question as to the best place
in which to house them. In most habitable
dwellings there is an attic or empty room in the roof
or upper story, with a window. That makes the
ideal " loft " for racing pigeons. The whole
or part of the window can be removed, and a
trap can quite easily be fitted to it. The
principle of the trap is that while no bird
can leave the loft unless the wires are purposely
removed, any bird returning can push its way
back through the wires at will. The trap must
possess a ledge on the outside upon which the

homing bird can alight, and another ledge on
the interior side of the wires, upon which a few
tick-beans or maple-peas are scattered, so as
to attract the bird to push its way in. Needless
to say such a trap must be placed where it is
impossible for a cat to reach it and force his or
her way through the wires,—or the pigeons are lost.

The birds will probably have been ringed when
first hatched with the identification rings of the
National Union of Homing Pigeons, bearing the
initials, " N.U.H.P." and a number and date. If
the sportsman breeds his own birds from a pair of
prisoners he should ring them himself, as this
provides a means of identification in case they
are lost or stolen ; and also, if shot by a poacher
or keeper, will entail a heavy fine being imposed
on the offender by the magistrates. In addition,
should a bird by any chance turn out a first-class
flier it may be sold for a big sum if ringed, which
would not otherwise be the case. A record of
the ring numbers of all birds should be kept in a
memorandum book.

After the squeakers have got accustomed to
their loft and been fed there—the staple diet
being barley, tares, maple-peas, tick-beans, and
dari-seed—the trap may be left open and the
birds allowed outside, when they will take short

flights to the roofs of adjoining buildings and
return in due course to the loft. The furniture
of this need only be very simple. A few bracket-
perches against the walls, a set of " pigeon-
hole " nest-boxes which a boy can easily construct
out of boxes from the grocer, a good water-
fountain, so constructed as not to be liable to
fouling by the birds' droppings, are all the fittings
absolutely necessary. The birds will be fed on
the floor of the loft, and this should be scraped
and cleaned every day, and thoroughly washed
out with disinfectant at regular intervals.

When the birds are old enough to be trained
to return to their loft from a distance, a basket
is advisable as a means of carrying them ; though
the young pitmen in Northumberland usually
put each pigeon in a blue-paper sugar-bag and
carry them in their pockets.

Training birds is quite simple. On the first
occasion they should be placed in the basket,
shortly before their proper feeding-hour, and
taken to a distance of from half a mile to a mile,
if possible to a place within view of the loft-
window and its trap. All the birds being released
together, they will rise into the air and after
circling round for a few seconds until they get
their bearings, will make straight for home;

where they should find the trap open and their food awaiting them. Of course a fine bright day must be selected, with as little wind as possible, and that blowing from where they are released towards the loft. Gradually the distances may be increased until the birds will return from a distance of ten or fifteen miles, which will probably be sufficient for the purposes of the young sportsman.

If several of these living in the same neighbourhood keep each a few racing-pigeons, competitive races can easily be arranged. All the birds, of different owners, must be released from the same basket together, the distances to each owner's loft carefully measured on an ordnance-map, and someone left at home to take the exact time when each bird arrives back at its own loft and enters the trap : the various watches or clocks used showing, of course, exactly the same time. The bird that does the distance at the quickest rate of speed per mile will be the winner ; and the prize may be a pool or sweepstakes at a penny or threepence a dirb.

Taking a bird with you when on a fishing or other sporting expedition and sending a message home by it to say when you may be expected

back, is an interesting method of training. The
message must be written on a slip of thin paper
and enclosed in one of the light cylinders sold
for the purpose, and then clipped on the leg of
the bird to be released. In this way all sorts of
messages can be sent home, such as the result of
a cricket or football match, for instance ; and the
birds can be made of great practical use in cases
of illness or other emergency.

Of course someone must be on the watch for
a returning bird, so as to go to the loft and take
off the cylinder. An ingenious boy with a turn
for mechanics can easily fit up an electric bell
which will ring in the house when the bird alights
on the trap or pushes its way through the wires,
and thus announce its arrival.

4. TIPPLER-FLYING

The tippler is another interesting pigeon,
whose original home is Macclesfield, its peculiarity
being that when released from its loft it soars
into the sky and continues to fly round and round
for many hours at a time, sometimes so high
that glasses are required with which to watch
the birds, although they never go out of sight of
the loft. These birds should be kept as what is
called a " kit " of three or five pigeons, and the

F

best of these kits will sometimes fly from dawn to dark without once alighting. A white fantail pigeon should be kept with the tipplers, and put out on the roof of the loft when it is required to get the kit to come down for the night. The white bird attracts the tipplers at once and brings them promptly home.

Tipplers are very handsome birds, either blue or black or chestnut in colour with white spots, or white in colour spotted with chestnut, black, or blue. They are hardy and require little attention; but, of course, should not be let out on stormy or foggy days, as under such weather-conditions they have no desire to fly.

Competitions may be arranged between various owners for length of flying, each kit being released by his owner at a preconcerted hour, and the one that remains flying for the longest period being adjudged the winner. I believe the record for flying tipplers is nearly twenty hours in the air without a single bird in the kit once dropping; but, of course, the tyro is not likely to get birds of this class, as they are very valuable. Anything over twelve hours in the air may be considered good for a kit: but, of course, if any one bird out of any one kit drops during this period the kit would be disqualified in a competition.

5. HAWKING INSECTS WITH JACKDAWS

Most boys are fond of keeping bird pets, magpies and jackdaws for choice, and very interesting pets they make, until, as usually happens, they come to an untimely end. They do not as a rule lend themselves to providing their owner with sport.

A tame jackdaw, however, will learn to sit upon its owner's fist and submit to be carried round the walls of a hut or garden-house which at night abounds in earwigs and other insects. An electric torch should be carried and shone upon the earwig, when the bird will promptly pick it off the wall with one incredibly sharp dig of its powerful beak and swallow it head foremost.

One of the Reserve Highland Battalions in a Scottish camp during the late war had such a pet jackdaw, which frequented the officers' mess and was not too popular with "dug-out" field-officers, whose eyeglasses it removed from the writing-tables and dropped into waste-paper baskets; while it earned further dislike from its habit of making sudden descents on the tables at meal-times and plunging its beak deep into the butter. The Adjutant, however, stood " Jock's " friend and used to take him off after mess to the Colonel's orderly-hut hawking earwigs, returning an hour or so later to announce the bag as " fifty-six earwigs and a brace of spiders," or something of that sort.

Birds like magpies and jackdaws, especially the latter, should—if taken at the proper age and correctly tamed and treated—never require to be confined or to have their wings " clipped." They should have a definite roosting-place somewhere inaccessible to prowling cats. Where there are no cats, an open box filled with sand, with a perch above it, and clean water always kept in a glass receptacle at one end of the box, makes as good a roosting-place as any ; but if cats are to be feared, an open cage, without a door, should be hung up in a sheltered place, where the bird can always reach it, but the cat never. Food and water should be placed there, and the jackdaw will always recognize it as home, and retire to it on all suitable occasions, if left the full use of its wings. In order to accustom a bird to its home, whether box or cage, it should invariably be fed there with a few strips of raw meat once a day.

If it is necessary—and safe—to prevent a young bird's flying away when first caught, instead of the barbarous plan of clipping the wing, which ruins its appearance, proceed as follows :

Spread out the wing and taking the quill feathers carefully strip the broad side of two out of every three, beginning with the second and third from the outside. This is a much more sightly and sensible plan than " clipping " the wing, and will effectually prevent the bird from flying. By the time it has moulted and acquired fresh feathers, the bird, if properly treated by its owner, will have ceased to want to fly away for good. It may, next spring, go off and seek a mate and rear a brood or two of young ones ; but when the breeding season is over, " fed-up " with family cares, it is pretty certain to return to its home. I knew one jackdaw that did so for nine seasons, and was only killed this year by a new cat. " Peter's " wings were never interfered with and he would fly for miles accompanying his master's children to the moors or to school. He flew about the village all these years and would call to people he knew from the roof of the butcher's shop that was his home ; but he was often on the counter, too, inquisitively examining the

customers' purchases as they were packed up.
He retired to the ruins of a neighbouring feudal
castle for breeding purposes, but looked in at
home every now and then to see how things were
going in his absence ; and nine months of the year
he roosted in the cage nailed against the stable-
wall.   On his return from rearing his ninth family,
however, a strange cat, who knew not Peter,
had been introduced—and the rest is silence !

IV : SPORTS REQUIRING A GUN
OR RIFLE

PRELIMINARY NOTES

I HAVE no intention of going at all deeply into the subject of shooting ; first, because the youthful sportsman for whom I am more particularly writing is not likely to possess either a gun or the right of shooting, and second, because if he does he will probably have someone to teach him how to use it better than any book can.

Still, of course, any boy should know how to handle firearms with safety to himself and others, and also how to kill birds and animals surely and humanely ; and most country boys will have, at any rate, occasional opportunities of shooting something in the way of " game " with a borrowed gun or a rook-and-rabbit rifle.

It is to be presumed that whoever lends him these will instruct him how to load, aim, and use them, and also compel him to clean the weapons properly after use. There are, however, some general hints which he will be all the better for seeing in black-and-white ; and I propose therefore to set them down here, so that he may refresh his memory from these pages before he goes out to shoot, and re-read them after the day's sport to see whether, by any chance, he has omitted any of these absolutely necessary precautions against accidents, and make a mental note not to do so in the future.

Since no boy of the present generation is at all likely to be given a muzzle-loading gun to shoot with, as was the writer's case, the first thing a boy should be taught is that he should never have his gun loaded except when there is a reasonable certainty that he is going to shoot something in the shape of game at once. It follows, therefore, not only that a gun should never be taken indoors with the cartridges in its chambers, but that it should never be laid down or stood against a wall unless the cartridges have been removed.

If a stile has to be crossed or a hedge climbed, the first thing to do is to remove the cartridges ; and a loaded gun should never be passed to another person to hand over an obstacle. Even if the hammers are down or the safety-bolt on, this must be the invariable rule. And when rough ground is to be crossed where there is no chance of shooting anything it is better to unload the gun than to put on the safety-bolt ; though the latter may be used in crossing rough ground where game may be expected to get up.

An unloaded gun can kill or injure no one : not-
withstanding which undoubted fact, there is
much truth in the *obiter dictum* of an old lady of
my acquaintance, that " a gun will go off, loaded
or not."

Having learnt that no real time is lost and no
real chance of killing game likely to be missed
through loss of the few seconds required to load
or unload a gun, the next thing the youthful
sportsman must master is the carrying a gun
safely. As Sir Ralph Payne-Gallwey says in his
Letters to Young Shooters which every boy should
read, "There are many ways of carrying a gun
dangerously, but only *one* way of carrying it *safely*,
as far as I know, and that is to hold it so that,
if fired by accident or intention, the charge
could not possibly cause injury to any living
thing except the game you wish to kill."

The " only *one* way " to carry a loaded gun
is the same way as that of carrying an unloaded
gun. The muzzle of the gun must point either
to the sky or directly towards the ground. If
it does not do so it is not safe, either to its carrier
or to any human being within 150 yards. If
the sportsman is rook- or pigeon-shooting the
muzzle must point skywards; if rabbits are the
game then it must point earthwards. For the

former the gun should be held athwart the body, the muzzle high across the left breast pointing well forward. For the latter, hold the butt between the elbow and the right side, the left hand well forward along the barrel, and the muzzle pointing to the front and well down. If game is not immediately expected, the gun, for a change, may be safely carried resting on the *right* shoulder, with the top rib of the barrel downwards on the shoulder. This will point the muzzle towards the sky.

The *great* aim of a young shooter should be to become a good shot ; but his *first* aim should be to become a safe shot. And he should remember that the eyes of everybody when he is in the field are directed upon him to ascertain the latter fact, and to a much less extent to discover whether he can hit the game at which he fires. If he fails to satisfy the observer on the first head it is precious little shooting he is likely to enjoy. I need hardly say that any boy seen to point his weapon in the direction of any human being, " in fun," should not only receive at competent hands the most severe thrashing that can possibly be administered to him ; but that he should not be allowed to touch either a gun or a rifle for at least twelve months ;

and perhaps not then until a sort of echo of the
first thrashing is given him to revive his memory
on the subject.

It is beyond the province of the written word
to teach a boy how to aim at a bird or beast
so as to kill it dead. That must perforce be left
to the instruction of the man who takes the boy
under his tutelage. But the ambition of every
boy who is allowed to shoot should be to *kill*
his game, whether on the ground or in the air,
so that it falls dead instantaneously,—and not as
a living but crippled bird or beast. The youthful
sportsman must be taught that it is a disgrace
to wing a bird or break the hind-legs of a rabbit ;
and that he must shoot to kill. It is far better
to miss game clean than merely to wound it ;
and if, by any chance, he should drop a wounded
bird, his gun should be taken away from him and
he should be made to find the bird or rabbit
(if above ground) before it is restored to him,
even if it takes him till nightfall to do so.

No boy should be allowed to follow game round
with the gun, but should be taught to put the
gun to the shoulder and fire at once. He should
never aim at anything he cannot clearly see and
distinguish for what it really is. And he should
never aim in any direction where there is cover

sufficient to conceal a human being, as a hedge or a haystack, however tempting the shot may be ; and in rabbit-shooting should never aim at the game while it is in the hedge, but wait until it bolts into the open, whether he knows that there is anybody on the other side of the hedge or not.

In this way he will always be a safe shot, and is very likely to become also a good, and perhaps a brilliant one into the bargain.

1. Rook- and Rabbit-Shooting

I have put these two forms of sport together because a rifle can be used for both, and is the most sporting weapon to employ ; although, of course, a shot-gun can equally be used for either, when no rifle is available.

To take the rook first. Only the young birds are killed when they are just fledged and sitting on the edges of their nests or at most have qualified as " branchers," birds that can just hop about on the adjoining twigs and smaller branches at the tops of the trees. Here the sight of the rook-rifle is laid directly on the bird as it sits at rest, and success is merely a question of correct alignment, depending upon good eyesight and absence of nervousness in the young shooter, at the moment of pressing—not *pulling*—the trigger. With a rifle the bird should either be killed outright or clean missed : with a shot-gun he may be wounded by stray pellets if the aim is not accurate, but will generally fall and be retrieved.

Rook-shooting is a late spring and early summer sport, and one that is very useful to enter the young sportsman ; who, being watched, will soon be judged by his elders as a promising or unpromising " gunner," according to how he handles his weapon and how he brings down his birds.

If he acquits himself well, he may be advanced to rabbit-shooting; also, in the early summer, as soon as the young rabbits are big enough to kill, and when, by lying quietly in one spot near which they will come out to feed at stated hours, he can obtain that " pot-shot," whether with rifle or gun, that will teach him to aim correctly and kill clean. Let no boy—or man either, for that matter—think that potting rabbits sitting close to their burrows is " unsportsmanlike." On the contrary it is the most sportsmanlike method of bringing them to hand, as there should be plenty of time to aim truly and thus kill them outright, whereas " snapping " them with a shot-gun would probably mean that they would escape wounded into the adjacent burrow, there to die a miserable and lingering death : which no true sportsman can desire.

Once the young shooter has killed a few rooks and rabbits in this way and acquired confidence in his eyesight and the use of his weapon, it will be time enough to let him aim at the moving target ; but here he passes out of the purview of this book, and will find himself in the hands of a keeper or adult of some sort, who for his own credit and safety's sake will see that he learns what no book can hope to teach.

2. SPARROW- AND STARLING-SHOOTING

This is a very minor form of sport, but not without its pleasures. A shot-gun must be used, and cartridges loaded with "dust shot": Number 10, which gives 1,726 pellets to the ounce, is the best.

Here the idea is to fire "into the brown" of a flock of sparrows feeding on the ground, or of a flock of starlings flying low on the way to the particular coppice or wood or osier-bed that they may have selected for a roosting-place during the autumn.

To use larger shot would be to spoil the birds for the table, and starlings are not half bad when roasted or made into pies, provided that their heads are cut off with a sharp-bladed knife directly they are killed. If this be not done they acquire a bitter taste that is extremely unpalatable.

The young shooter must exercise a certain amount of woodcraft in this pursuit. It may be easy to attract a crowd of house-sparrows to a given spot by strewing food about, the while he lies in ambush with a gun ; but starlings cannot be managed in this way. The flights must be watched, night after night, and will be found to take place over exactly the same tract of land each evening, a little before sunset. The sportsman should take up a position under the shelter of some trees a few minutes before the earliest flight is due, and having taken his toll of that, wait patiently until the next following flight. If the spot be well-chosen he should manage to make quite a respectable bag each night during the pre-Christmas period ; shortly after which they begin to change their venue and the sport of starling-shooting may be considered over for the year.

3. Wood Pigeon-Shooting

Wood pigeons by their numbers and the destruction they work have now in the British

Isles come to be reckoned as much vermin as rats and house-sparrows. Their numbers are, like those of the starling, recruited annually by the flocks that migrate to England from the Continent of Europe ; and their slaughter has become so meritorious that it should be rewarded by a payment *per capitem*, as is the case in many places with sparrows and rats.

Wood pigeon-shooting calls probably for the highest skill that the young shooter will be expected to display : for the wood pigeon is not only a wary bird but his strong quills will turn the shot and often leave him scatheless if hit anywhere but in the head or immediately from below and behind.

Woodcraft is necessary here. In ordinary open weather the wood or copse in which they roost must be noted and a position taken up some time before they are likely to fly into it for the night. If the wind is blowing strongly into such a wood they are not likely to visit it, or, if it be a large wood, only on the more sheltered side. The sportsman should take up position under some evergreen tree, such as a holly or fir, commanding a view of adjoining trees in which the birds are fond of roosting, like larches. They are apt to come in very quietly in parties of five or six, but usually make a certain amount of noise with their wings on settling, which announces their arrival to the hidden gunner. Immediately they settle they peer round and down to discover whether any foe is at hand. Their sight is extraordinarily keen and the slightest movement on the part of the waiting sportsman will be at once detected and the birds depart in a body. Curiously enough they seem to be almost deaf, or at least very hard of hearing, and no noise disturbs them : even the report of the gun that has killed one of their number they appear unable to locate, and after flying about bewildered for a few minutes, the unharmed birds will frequently settle and afford another shot : that is, if the sportsman remains in concealment, and does not emerge to pick up any bird he happens to have dropped.

Method of
setting up a Decoy
Pigeon with wire netting

G

During hard weather wood pigeons can be killed on their feeding grounds, say in the turnip-fields, for they are extremely fond of turnip-tops when other food fails them. In this case some sort of shelter must be contrived where a shot can be got at a feeding bird. Directly a pigeon is killed he should be wired according to the plan shown in the illustration, or set up somehow with a forked stick to look as if he were still alive and still feeding on turnip-tops. This will speedily attract another passing wood-pigeon to alight near by, and if it be shot it can be set up in the same manner at a little distance from the first one, but still within range of the shooter.

During the late summer months a hedgerow-ash is a favourite place for a solitary pigeon to alight : and a gun concealed in the ditch or hedge-row within sight and range of the tree will often be able to pick off a brace or two in the course of an afternoon.

Wood-pigeons, of course, are excellent eating, especially after they have been feeding on beech-mast ; and the boy who shoots them should be able to trade them to the cook or housekeeper for at least enough to keep him in the cartridges he expends on shooting them.

The young shooter must be careful to distinguish

between wood-pigeons and homing-pigeons, as the killing of the latter is very properly a serious offence, rarely punished by a smaller fine than £5, with the value of the dead bird to make good in addition.

4. SHOOTING GAME WITH A BOW AND ARROWS

Where the gun is out of the question, rooks, rabbits, and wood pigeons may be killed in a truly sportsmanlike manner with a bow and arrows, after the manner of Robin Hood and those of our ancestors who won the Battle of Creçy.

There are two kinds of bows, of course, the cross-bow and the long-bow. As a boy, I used to make my own cross-bows with a block of wood grooved to hold the " bolt," a piece of bent cane and the string, fitting into its notch ; and could bring down a sitting bird " as dead as any nail that is in any door," four or five times out of ten. I have often wondered that the modern " Sports Emporiums," do not offer cross-bows for sale, since they are simple and effective, should not be expensive (mine never cost me more than sixpence apiece, if I remember rightly) and moreover harmless to human beings, as, unless they caught a person a " bat in the eye " they could do no damage to anything except a bird ; the bolt (or " bird-bolt " as it is still called in heraldry) being a shaft of wood furnished with a knob of hard, dried clay instead of a metal point like the long-bow arrow. This is intended, of course, to pierce its victim ; whereas the " bird-bolt " was meant to stun or fell the object aimed at.

I have a hazy recollection of making long-bows also, but do not remember that they were nearly so effective as the cross-bow. Fortunately the modern youth need not make his own long-bows, since, thanks to the fact that archery is still a recognized, though somewhat recondite, pastime, good bows and efficient arrows can still be purchased from the " Sports Emporiums."

Rooks, pigeons, and rabbits can all be killed with the long-bow ; in fact, sportsmen like Mr. Straker and Dr. Peard have killed in India and the Argentine respectively very many descriptions of game with no other weapon. The boy with no gun, but that hypothetical rich uncle to whom I have previously referred, might do worse than take his birthday or Christmas present out in the shape of a good bow and half a dozen arrows.

In case the uncle should not happen to be a member of the Royal Toxophilite Society, let me recommend him to buy a good " ladies' " bow of " self-lance " or " three-piece yew, fustic and hickory " for his nephew, and six " straight " arrows, which ought to suffice any but the most careless, thriftless nephew. A boy should be able to shoot birds and rabbits without " tips," or " bracers," up to a distance of at least 50 yards, which is a greater distance than he could kill them with were he using a gun.

Stone-throwing, either with the hand or by means of a sling, and the use of catapults should be discouraged in young sportsmen, as they are, very properly, illegal, and although much skill is necessary to bring down small birds in either manner, the danger of blinding some unsuspected human being, or breaking a window, is so great and so frequent that no true sportsman will wish to incur it.

V : SPORT WITH FISHES

1. WIRING PIKE AND JACK

IN England a small pike is called a jack and
a large jack is called a pike ; and that is
all the difference there is " to it.'' Angling
for pike is a very fine sport in itself, but for the
purposes of this book angling in all its branches
ranks as a Major Sport. There are, however,
many rivers and streams where the pike is
discountenanced and called such harsh and
uncomplimentary names as " fresh-water shark,"
and so on. In these waters nothing but game
fish—trout and grayling—are esteemed ; and if
any pike are suspected of haunting them, keepers
and water-bailiffs are enjoined to have them out
of it—by foul means (from the pike-angler's
point of view) for preference.

Periodically, such rivers are netted at considerable expense, and jack and pike ruthlessly removed ; while, when this is not feasible, the keepers do their best to wire, and grapple or " snatch " the pike out of the water so jealously reserved to game fish.

It is in such streams that the minor sportsman may, by arrangement, enjoy his sport without a rod : indeed, no one who hasn't paid his 25 guineas entrance fee plus some other large number of guineas as annual subscription dare be seen, rod-in-hand, within a couple of fields of the waterside. If, however, the young sportsman will take the trouble to propitiate the keeper or the secretary of the club he will have little difficulty in obtaining permission to get out a pike in the best way he can devise.

On a hot summer day he will find this best way by means of a wire. Pike are fond of basking in the stream just below the surface on such days, and will lie alongside a weed-bed or under the bank for hours at a time, apparently sound asleep. It is in such a situation that they may most easily be wired.

The apparatus consists of, first, a wire noose like a rabbit-snare and running as easily. This should be fastened to a piece of water-cord about two feet in length, and the water-cord in its turn

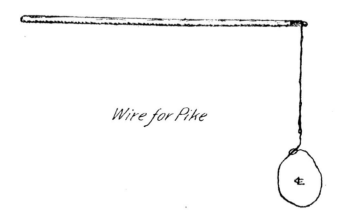

Wire for Pike

to a light but strong six-foot pole. The method
to be pursued is this : having " spotted " your
pike enjoying his afternoon nap, the pole must
be very slowly and carefully extended over the
water up-stream of the fish until the wire noose
is just in front of and in a line with it. The
noose is then gently lowered into the water and
allowed to come down with the stream until it
encircles the pike. Even if it touches the fish
he will probably take no notice—though if you
work up from behind, as can often be done, the
wire must not touch him or he'll be off like a shot.
If the noose doesn't go over the pike at the first
attempt—sometimes it doesn't—let it go past
slowly at the same pace as the current, and take
it quietly out below and try again. The fish is

not likely to be alarmed if you move it quietly. When it does go over the head wait until it gets to about half the length of the body, perhaps a trifle nearer the head than the tail ; and then, with a sharp jerk, heave the fish out on the bank over your head.

If it is at all a big fish knock it on the head with a stone or a " priest "—as the sort of special constable's baton sold for killing fish is called—before attempting to handle it ; for pike have formidable teeth and do not scruple to use them upon human fingers.

Another way in which pike may be caught without a rod and line is by " grappling " for them. A triangle or treble, consisting of three large hooks in one, rather like the flukes of an anchor, is attached to a length of strong fishing-line with some lead just above the treble to weight it. This can only be used from a place of vantage such as the parapet of a bridge, or a rock overlooking a deep part of the stream. When the pike is discovered lying by its weed-bed the grapple is thrown out and allowed to sink just beside it and on the side of the fish furthest from the " grappler." When the latter sees or feels that the triangle is alongside and just below the level of the fish, he gives the line

a sharp jerk that drives one or more of the barbs
into the side of the fish and then hangs on like
grim death until he can drag the pike ashore—
often, if it is of any size, after a lively and exciting
struggle.

It cannot be denied that there are elements
of both skill and sport in these methods of cap-
turing pike in all waters where they are regarded
as vermin. In water where they are angled for,
and highly esteemed for their sport-giving
properties to fishermen who spin or live-bait for
them, such methods would amount to poaching
and must on no account be pursued.

2. Sniggling and Spearing Eels

Here again the young sportsman must be careful
to avoid the suspicion of being a poacher, and
make sure that both he and his methods have
the approval of the owner or lessee of the water
before putting them into practice : though so
far as skill goes, both sniggling and spearing eels
require more of it than angling for them does.
Trapping them in eel-buckets, of course, provides
no " sport " at all, and is only justifiable as a commercial expedient for supplying the markets.
Night-lining is a veritable form of poaching, and
does great harm ; as trout and other fish are

taken on the night-lines and having gorged the bait must necessarily be destroyed whether in season or out of season. Night-lines therefore are taboo.

Warm summer-weather is suitable for sniggling, and a long wand or stick, of about six feet, with a handle at one end is required, as well as a strong needle and a length of fishing-line—three or four yards should suffice. The line is attached to the needle by being whipped round it from the eye to about half-way down, and a worm is then threaded on the needle from tail to head. The point of the needle is then stuck into the end of the handle of the wand or stick, the bight of the line being retained in the sniggler's left hand. This leaves the right hand free to manipulate the wand, which should be placed in the water and guided gently to all such places as eels may frequent : holes in the banks, apertures in camp-shedding, crevices of rocks and stones and so forth.

In this way the worm is offered to any eel that may chance to be at home and anhungered. If it notices the worm it will promptly seize it, thus releasing the needle from the handle of the stick, which can be pulled up and cast upon the bank. The line can be transferred to the right hand and after the eel has been allowed a couple of minutes to gorge the worm, the sniggler takes a hand and by keeping up a strong un-relaxing pull will eventually persuade the eel to leave its place of refuge and come out on the bank.

Sniggling-tackle

The strong, steady pull is the secret : jerks and tugs with the inevitable intervening slackening of the line are fatal to success. Directly the eel is safe on the bank at some distance from the water, cut its head nearly but not quite off from the back and extract the needle.

Most success in spearing eels is obtainable when the water is clear enough for the eels to be seen lying or moving on the bottom ; and in deeper water when the bubbles that rise to the surface, where they are blowing in the mud, give an indication of whereabouts they are. An eel-spearhead, which any blacksmith can make for you, should have five prongs, three large and barbed, and the spaces between these filled with smaller and shorter prongs unbarbed : the whole being attached to a pole of sufficient length for the water to be operated in. Of course in rivers and ponds known to abound in eels, it is possible to spear for them at hazard : stabbing the mud in winter and the weed-beds in summer, and taking whatever fortune the gods may provide.

3. MINNOW- AND GUDGEON-FISHING

Minnows are usually sought to be taken alive for the purpose of being used as live-bait for pike, or in spinning for salmon and trout, or perch and jack. The young sportsman may be able to make a little pocket-money by collecting sufficient to sell to some more fortunate major sportsman. The same may be said of the gudgeon ; although both these small fish make excellent eating if cooked like white-bait. Minnows may, of course, be angled for with a very small hook and a fragment of worm attached by a line to the end of a hazel-rod ; but a more wholesale way of securing them in any numbers is by the use of a minnow-net. Special minnow-nets are sold, but an ordinary landing-net lined with a piece of thin sacking or even coarse muslin can be made to serve.

Minnow-net

A shoal of minnows having been observed, either in the stream during the summer or in ditches and runners during the winter months, the net should be sunk above or below it and the little fish frightened into it by splashing gently behind them with a stick or punt-paddle. As

soon as a few are seen in or over the net it should
be lifted and these removed to a bucket half-filled
with water, or a live-bait can—if one is available
—and the netting process repeated as before.

Gudgeon, unfortunately, are not to be caught
in this simple way, but must be angled for with rod
and line, though a rake may be required to stir
up the bottom and set them on the feed—an
ordinary garden-rake will do the trick. Fine
float-tackle with a very small float, a small hook
with a red-painted shank and part of a worm, is
all that is required ; it is not necessary to have
a reel and running line, though it is advisable.
A line fastened to a hazel-wand will be sufficient,
provided the rest of the tackling is as prescribed ;
and a shot placed about 4 inches above the hook
to steady the worm. Of course more shot may
be required if there is any considerable current.

4. CRAY-FISH CATCHING

The cray-fish is a sort of miniature fresh-
water lobster found in chalk-streams and many
other kinds of water, even in ponds and reservoirs.

It can be angled for with a worm, and when
drawn to the bank will usually walk ashore
hugging the worm and wearing a ludicrous look of
surprise at the experience it is undergoing.

However, not many cray-fish can be caught in this way, and a better plan is to use the baited basket. A fairly deep basket with a handle is required, and to the handle must be attached a cord. The bottom of the basket must be weighted with a stone, and a bit of fairly high liver fastened to the bottom makes the most attractive bait. Thus equipped, the cray-fish catcher proceeds to the water haunted by these little scavengers of fresh-water brooks, and sinks his basket to the bottom. After the lapse of sufficient time, or where—the water being clear—he can see that a number of cray-fish have swarmed into the basket, he must haul up very rapidly, as otherwise they will scramble out with remarkable rapidity, and escape into the river before the basket can be swung ashore.

Cray-fish are, of course, a table delicacy and make an excellent breakfast dish, served cold with mayonnaise sauce. They turn to a delicate pink when boiled, though their natural colour is a brownish-olive.

VI: MISCELLANEOUS SPORTS

1. FINDING THE EGGS OF CERTAIN BIRDS

BIRDS-NESTING is, of course, a sort of sport in itself which possesses an extensive literature of its own; and where the object is merely to discover and identify the nests and eggs of different species without robbing them it is harmless enough, and useful as adding to the sum of individual Nature knowledge.

In this sub-section, however, I shall only indicate the method of finding the eggs of two common birds, because they are both good for human food, and are indeed counted as delicacies by *gourmets*. These are the lapwing and the moor-hen: the one found on ploughed fields and marshy land and frequently along the margins of lakes; the other by the sides of brooks and streams and inland ponds.

Most sportsmen know the appearance of a plover's egg; but not everyone knows an infallible method of finding the nests. Peewits may be noted feeding in the pastures and wheeling overhead with plaintive cries and much "fanning" of their wings; but the nests on the ground will remain invisible to the inexpert searcher. These nests are little more than what ornithologists call "scrapes," on the bare ground, sometimes sparsely lined with grass, bents, or ore-weed, according to the locality in which they are found. They are usually slightly elevated above the surrounding level, but less frequently may be found in a depression, such as a hoof-mark. Where the ground is at all stony it is not easy to distinguish the three or four pyriform eggs, varying in ground colour from brownish or yellowish-olive to olive green, thickly blotched and spotted with dark brown or almost black markings.

If only a solitary green-plover or at most a pair are noted in a good-sized meadow it is hardly worth while trying to find the nest ; and a move should be made to some enclosure where a dozen or so birds are visible. If this be an arable field before it has been sown or planted, a good plan is to walk down one furrow and back up the next, keeping to the crown of the furrow, walking slowly, and allowing the eyes to sweep the ground immediately in front of the feet as they advance.

Most persons are apt to look too far ahead : the proper thing is to look just far enough in

front to be able to stop before the foot treads on
the eggs.

In meadows and pastures an entirely different
plan of searching for plovers' eggs must be
adopted, if success is to be achieved. A reference
to the accompanying illustration will explain the
system. A survey of the field must be made

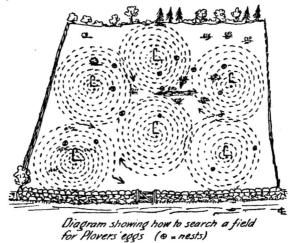

Diagram showing how to search a field
for Plovers' eggs (⊕ = nests)

roughly by eye and the number of " beats " it
will take to cover it loosely estimated. Taking a
square of about 25 yards by 25 yards, the searcher
should proceed to its centre and fix his walking-
stick upright in the ground. He should then
commence to walk round and round the stick,
from left to right, in an ever-increasing and

widening spiral. He must walk slowly, his eyes fixed upon the ground just in front of his right foot, head very slightly inclined to the right so as to be continuously conscious out of the tail of his right eye of the position of the walking-stick. As he gets farther and farther from this he should note any small " landmark " which he passes : a stone, piece of wood, mole-heap, hoof-mark, and so on—so as to avoid covering more than a small portion of the same ground twice. When he judges that he is about 15 yards from the stick on the side nearest the next square to be beaten, he should make a mark on the ground, go and fetch the stick, walk 15 yards farther on, insert the stick in the ground as before, and repeat the spiral tour. In this way it is impossible to miss a single nest, and often the nests of larks and other ground-building birds will also be found ; and the whole field can be searched and covered. More nests will be found towards its centre than near the boundaries.

If the nest, when found, contains two or three eggs, one or two may be taken, that is in a country where it is not suspected that regular search for plovers' eggs is carried on ; but if four eggs, or sometimes even three, are found with the pointed ends turned towards the centre, and especially if these are warm to the touch as though the sitting bird has just left them, it will be safer to leave them in peace ; as, especially if a little late in the season, they are almost certain to be unfit for food. If plovers' eggs are very much needed one egg may be taken to a little distance and broken and if found to be fresh two more can be removed ; but one should always be left.

I have known dogs trained to find plovers' nests, both spaniels and Highland terriers ; but they will both point larks' nests, and of course those of the meadow-pipit or titlark, owing to their high " gamey " scent, are irresistible to most sporting dogs.

Moor-hens' eggs are just as good to eat as those of the lapwing, and their nests are very much easier to find. The searcher must be prepared to wade for them, however, and will find an otter-pole or a landing-net-handle invaluable. Moor-hens lay from six to ten eggs, and when more than six are found it is always advisable to remove one to a distance and test it, so as to avoid taking those hard-set. The nest itself is a large structure placed just above the water-level and conspicious by reason of the material of flags and dried water-weeds of which it is built. Almost every little brook and runner and field-pond has its moor-hen's nest, and if they are within easy access of home they may be so nursed as to provide a large number of eggs, if they are visited every two or three days and two or three eggs only removed at each visit. They are clay-coloured as to the ground hue, with spots and specks of reddish and purplish brown.

Moor-hens often have three broods during the season, never less than two, so that they may well be laid under contribution to supply a delicacy for the breakfast-table.

2. VIPER-KILLING

In all parts of Great Britain the one poisonous reptile of its fauna is to be found in the shape of the viper or adder, as it is very commonly called. Vipers vary a great deal in size and colour, but there are but two other reptiles for which the tyro may mistake them : namely, the harmless grass-snake and the blind-worm or slow-worm, which is in reality a lizard and not a serpent. But neither of these has the distinctive sign of the viper : a dark " V "-shaped mark upon the head, which no viper is without.

In some parts, chiefly on bare mountain-sides and vast tracks of land like the New Forest, they may be found in great numbers, on any sunny day in spring and early summer, basking in the welcome heat ; and it is here that the viper-hunter should look for them.

Most dogs dislike snakes and some few will kill them ; but it is not very safe to encourage them to try. The bite of a full-grown viper at the top of his form will paralyze, if not kill, a terrier, while if the viper bites even a hound or big dog in the throat he may be choked to death by the resultant swelling before aid can be given.

Dogs may be used to find vipers in heathery places and should be taught to stand back and bark or bay them until their masters can come up and slay them. But in case of accident, if a dog be taken out for this sport, a small bottle containing the following mixture should be carried : 6 oz. of olive oil mixed with 90 drops of sal-volatile. If the dog is bitten, a drench of about a sixth of this mixture (more if the dog is a large one) should at once be administered, and the actual wound also rubbed with the mixture. The treatment should be repeated after six hours.

The best implement for catching vipers is a cleft stick, or one with a narrow fork, by which they can be pinned to the ground just behind the head. Then, as they say in Cornwall, " stank 'pon its head " with the heel of a steel-shod shoe or kill it with a blow from a metal-shod stick. The Scriptural method of " bruising the serpent's head " is still the best ; but be careful the serpent does not also scripturally " bruise your heel " while you are doing it. It is here that the value of the forked stick to hold the head in place becomes manifest.

3. MILLIPEDE-RACING

All the sports previously dealt with are out-door sports, and subject more or less to fine-weather conditions. Millipede-racing is an indoor pastime and may be enjoyed on the inevitable wet day that comes sooner or later during the finest summer. Apart from that it may be described as the most minor of all minor sports ; but there is some fun in it not-withstanding, and no element of cruelty to the millipede.

There are many millipedes, but so far as I have discovered only one racing millipede. This is known to naturalists as *Julus terrestris*, and may be looked for and found in large numbers under stones, decaying wood, bark, or the roots of plants, under heaps of leaf-mould, and not infrequently climbing about porches and doors in damp weather. It is a very handsome little beast about an inch in length, being shiny black on the back, and bright silver underneath, with the softest of silken legs of a pale fawn colour. It curls up in a small ring when at rest, and races best on a polished table-top.

Racing Millipede (Julus terrestris) Life-size

All that is required is for each owner to select his *Julus terrestris*, which are then placed in a row at one end of the table, a barrier or starting gate in the shape of a foot rule being placed before them, and the edge of the table and each side of the " course " blocked with books to prevent their " bolting." Once they start, on the removal of the ruler, they go like steam, with occasional brief pauses for enquiries, probably ; and a pool or sweepstakes can be arranged, the owner of the one that reaches the other end of the table first taking the pool. They will sometimes cross and foul one another, and a good plan is to lay down lathes lengthways so that they cannot do this, after the manner in which dog-racing grounds are laid out, and with a similar object in view. If it is proposed to keep

an outstanding racer it should be placed in a
dark box and fed upon bulbs and roots.

4. BEETLE-FIGHTING

This is another sport that may be enjoyed
indoors if desired : the beetles employed being
the *Soldier Beetle* and the *Sailor Beetle*.
The one is brick-red in colour and the other
navy-blue, circumstances that probably sug-
gested their English names. They are not found
in every part of the country ; but in the New
Forest both abound. They appear to hate each
other with a most virulent hatred ; and never
do a soldier beetle and a sailor beetle meet
without fighting to the death. Neither of them
will fight one of its own kind, and thus it is quite
safe to put a number of soldier (or sailor) beetles
into a box together, but not to mix them—the
" sailors " with the " soldiers." Both are nearly
the same size and shape and it is even betting which
of any two specimens will be first killed in a fight.

It is these peculiar properties, coupled with the
ferocity with which they fight to the death,
that entitles them to a place among the sporting
creatures of the world : and like fighting-cocks
they engage in combat entirely for their own
enjoyment and without the slightest reference to

the human beings who may derive amusement from their contests.

Fighting these beetles may be arranged precisely on the old lines that regulated a main of cocks under Westminster Rules. An odd number of beetles of either species should be chosen, either 11, 21, or 61, and if there should be any over they may be matched in separate combats or bye-battles. The sportsman should first spin a coin for choice of colour—Soldier or Sailor—unless they can otherwise agree upon the point. A shallow circular " pit " about six inches in diameter must be provided : the cover of a Camembert-cheese box ; or the box itself slightly cut down makes an excellent beetle-pit.

Into this a beetle of each species is placed, and they are left to fight it out, the one that lives longest being accounted the winner as in cock-fighting : in fact, all the rules of cock-fighting apply excellently well to beetle-fighting. The stakes for boys—if stakes there must be—may be a penny a battle and sixpence the odd or main ; or any other agreed sum. Sportsmen " of a larger growth " can, of course, gamble to their hearts' content on the result of a main of beetles.

VII: SOME MAJOR FIELD SPORTS

IN WHICH YOUNG SPORTSMEN MAY TAKE PART

PRELIMINARY NOTES

ALTHOUGH a pony, a gun, or a fly-rod be denied the youthful or impecunious sportsman for whom this book is chiefly written, a majority of them may, as occasion offers, take some small part in the greater field-sports for which Great Britain has always been famous : sports which have made the British race what it is, and contributed so much to the success of its members all the world over, and in every walk in life. These Major Field Sports, as I will venture to call them, are : Hunting in its several branches, Coursing, Fishing, and Shooting. In all these there is room as an onlooker, when the opportunity presents itself, for the boy or youth or unmoneyed man who knows how to conduct himself so as not to interfere with the sport enjoyed by his elders, and, so far as their pockets go, at any rate, his betters. He may, in fact, go a great deal farther, and in place of being merely tolerated as an inoffensive observer, prove himself of real use in the hunting-field, at a coursing meeting, with the guns, or by the riverside, provided that he be inspired by the real sportsmanlike feelings which I have throughout these pages endeavoured to inculcate ; and be willing to make himself of actual use to the hunting- and shooting-men, anglers, or coursers who permit him to accompany them in their pursuit of the various and varied pleasures of the chase.

Any old clothes will do for hunting on foot, but a few hints on dress may be advisable. Woollen shirts and stockings should invariably be worn, and in arable countries boots instead of shoes, which often let small stones and clods of earth get inside the soles, and so stop the runner abruptly. In a grass country this does not occur so often, and shoes may be worn ; but stout leather brogues protect the feet and are better in the long run than the canvas running-shoes sometimes worn for lightness' sake.

A sweater is preferable to a coat, and running-knickers may be worn if liked : while in fair weather a cap may be dispensed with by the whole-hearted follower of beagles and basset-hounds who proposes to depend on his running and staying powers to see the sport. When out with the harriers or the fox-hounds a hat or cap should be worn, and in the former case a stick or jumping-pole may be carried : the latter is indispensable in a dyke country.

For otter-hunting woollen clothes are indispensable, as most boys will want to enter the water ; and if they are so clad it will do them no harm to do so, provided they don't sit or lie about in their wet garments, but keep moving until they have an opportunity to change into dry things. A flannel shirt and suit and woollen hose, with shoes rather than boots, as the former hold less water than the latter, is the costume indicated ; and an otter-pole of ash or bamboo, of a length and weight proportioned to the young sportsman's size, are all the equipment he will require. On the pole he will be proud to cut a notch whenever he is present at a kill ; and the record thus made will serve him as a reminder of many pleasant, healthful days spent by the waterside in the pursuit of what is perhaps the most genuine and legitimate as it is undoubtedly the oldest of all organized British Sports.

1. IN THE HUNTING FIELD

Fox-Hunting

{The presence of " foot-people " (opprobrious term !) in the hunting-field has probably caused more bad language than anything else, save that

of a " hair-dresser " riding over hounds ; and
chiefly for the reason that they do not know where
to place themselves so as to see something of
the sport without running the risk of heading the
fox ; and that, when they have or have not done
so, but have undoubtedly seen it, they will not
keep silence ; but by crying aloud and shouting,
distract the attention of the pack, get hounds'
heads up and so off the scent, and not improbably
ruin a promising run or even lose the huntsman
his fox.

Now this is precisely where the young sportsman, and the sportsman with insufficient means
to enable him to ride to hounds, can be of
incalculable service to the hunt, if they will but
take the pains to learn what they may and may not
do, when they go to a meet, or follow the hunt
on foot. Every good and competent master of
hounds, and a majority of huntsmen also, know
the value of a " foot person " with a knowledge
of the country and of the habits of foxes or
hares, who comes out with their packs ; and once
they have ascertained his reliability, will not
hesitate to consult him when hounds for any of
many reasons are at fault. He can often set
them right when they have changed to a fresh
quarry ; or by pointing out the precise gap

through which it may have left a piece of bad
scenting ground save them valuable minutes in
getting on terms with the hunted animal. But
in order to do so they must know not only how
and when to " holloa, "—or, better still, to hold
up their hats or caps,—but also where to look
and where to be, at the psychological moment
when their services can be of most value to the
hunt.

At a meet of fox-hounds, the young sportsman
who wishes to qualify for the title of a keen and
willing hand will keep clear of the pack and not
try and coax them away from the huntsman and
whippers-in by offering them pieces of bread
or bits of biscuit. At the same time he should
be near enough to notice individual hounds and
can learn the names of many by watching those
that from time to time answer to the " rate "
of the hunt servants. A knowledge of the names
of the hounds in any pack will prove an excellent
beginning to the sportsman's education, and may
prove of great value in the field. If a boy who
has seen two or three couple of hounds pursuing
a line of their own, when the main body of the
pack is running in a contrary direction, is able
to give the huntsman or second whipper-in the
name of any of the hounds he has marked doing

so, the latter will know what deduction to make from the fact that an old and tried hound or some youngsters not yet thoroughly entered to the sport are on the scent of the hunted fox or that of an entirely fresh one.

The young sportsman who is to prove himself of value to his elders in the hunting-field must use his eyes to some effect, and his voice very sparingly. It is the noisy chattering groups of schoolboys that are such a nuisance in the hunting-field, and if the boy for whom I am writing is accompanied by others he should use his influence and set them a good example by not chattering or shouting himself, and especially by exhorting them to keep their tongues still.

When hounds move off to draw the first covert he should, on ascertaining which that is to be, reflect for a moment on such points as the direction and strength of the prevailing wind which will influence the huntsman as to the point from which he will commence to draw. All big coverts are drawn up-wind, that is, in the direction from which the wind is blowing at the time.

This is done in order, in case a fox be found, to let the widely-spreading pack quickly into the cry ; and in a small covert it is not so necessary. Once hounds have proclaimed a find the young

I

sportsman will naturally be anxious to see the fox break covert ; but he must not attempt to do so at the risk of heading him. To head a fox is the worst crime that can be committed in the hunting-field next to that of riding over a hound, and the boy—or man for that matter—who is guilty of it may expect to get the roughest side of the huntsman's tongue and to be greeted with sour looks the next time he goes to a meet.

With large coverts a fox may break at any place from which he has a point to make ; and as no definite rule can be laid down, so no definite information can be given as to the place at which a spectator, wishful to view the quarry away, may most profitably and harmlessly take up his position. The first whipper-in, in the case of all coverts, and also the second whipper-in in that of large coverts, will be sent to the spot or spots from which it is most likely the fox will break. If a young sportsman can, without danger of heading a fox, or that of being heartily cursed if he do so, follow either of these functionaries quickly and quietly to his post, and, standing motionless and silent behind them against a tree or boundary-wall, keep his ears and eyes open, he is very likely to be rewarded by a good view of the fox as he breaks. Let him remain silent and motion-

less until,—after the whipper-in has by " view-
holloa " or uplifted cap signalled the departure—
the huntsman and hounds are out-of-cover and
well away at his brush.

Then, while still refraining from shouting, he
may run to the nearest 'vantage point in order
to obtain a full view of the chase as it recedes into
the distance : or, if he proposes to follow on foot
and knows the country, he may decide for what
point—distant covert, main earth or what-not—
the quarry is making, and take his own way in that
direction by a mixed method of alternately
running and walking that with perseverance
will bring him, in more instances than he will
think probable until he tries it, near enough to
the death to witness the breaking-up of the
quarry and possibly to obtain on rare occasions
the trophy of a pad.

During a run of the sort disliked by steeple-
chasers, thrusters, or hard-riding dealers, who only
come out to show and sell horses, a slow hunting
run on a catchy scenting day, the young foot-
sportsman will be able to see a great deal of the
sport. He will learn to guide himself by the cry
of hounds borne melodiously on the breeze as
they bend towards him or travel farther afield,
although they may be out of sight. If he keeps

his eyes strained well forward he may judge by
the staring of cattle in the enclosures, the
wheeling of sheep, and finally by the gathering
and mobbing of the crows that will follow a
sinking fox, how the chase is progressing, when
he can no longer hear the cry of hounds nor see
the flying pack. I do not recommend him to
pay any attention to horsemen in the hunting
field: and especially are many of those who ride
in pink apt to be misleading guides. Of course
the young sportsman will have noted the colour
of the horse ridden by the huntsman, and if
he can clearly distinguish both they will be safe
guides to follow. A whipper-in may be actually
riding away from hounds for some purpose, and
a proportion of most modern fields will be doing
so without knowing it. Therefore, the cry of
hounds is undoubtedly his best guide in a blind
and wooded country, and he should always try to
keep down-wind of the hounds and the probable
line of the chase. He must remember, too, that
the majority of foxes will also travel down the
wind, that is, in the direction in which the wind
is blowing, or they will, for certain distances,
cheek the wind, or run with it blowing against
their flanks. Only for a short distance, with a safe
stronghold to be gained hard-by, will they as a

rule run up-wind ; except in a gale sufficiently strong to blow their brushes over their backs or so much to one side as to impede their progress.

The following of a fox-hunt on foot with a reasonable prospect of seeing more of the sport than is to be found at the meet or even when the fox breaks covert is thus seen not to be so difficult a matter after all. Old Peter Beckford in his *Thoughts on Hunting*—a book which no boy is too young nor any man too old to read and re-read if he wants to be a fox-hunter—says somewhere: "Every country is soon known ; and nine foxes out of ten, with the wind in the same quarter, will follow the same track. It is easy, therefore, for the whipper-in to cut short, and catch the hounds again ; at least it is so in the country where I hunt."

That was in Dorsetshire and a century since ; but that it is true, and that it applies to the foot-sportsman in not much lesser degree than to the whipper-in, may be shown by the experience of the present writer. He learnt the greater portion of the Duke of Beaufort's and the Berkeley counties in Gloucestershire and the borders of Wiltshire, including the lie of the land and the run of the foxes, in one season ; perfected his knowledge in a second season ; and, that he had mastered it, was shown by the fact that in his third season, that of 1913—1914, although in his forty-eighth year, he covered 2,089 miles on foot with both packs and was in at the death of 76 foxes. Younger and keener sportsmen may easily accomplish similar feats if so inclined ; but of course much depends upon the nature of the country in which their lines may be cast.

Once the foot-sportsman begins to run after the hounds he can easily be of use to huntsman and field. At the first three fences there is sure to be a press of horsemen eager to avoid a jump and anxious to have a gate opened or a pole removed from a gap. There is nothing derogatory in stopping for a moment to do this, and it may often occur in going from one covert to another to draw. A boy who sees barbed-wire unmarked by flag or board in a fence some horseman is going to jump, is bound to sing out, " 'Ware wire ! " at the top of his voice. He may also be able to help some good but unfortunate sportsman to catch his horse ; and, of course, if there is an accident, will always give up his own chances of further sport in order to be of help : by assisting to take a field-gate from its hinges, or going to summon a conveyance, or even a doctor, in serious cases. By such action he will speedily come to be regarded as a genuine sportsman, and his presence in the hunting-field on foot welcomed rather than tolerated.

Again, should hounds when running turn towards him, as they sometimes will—since fortune often favours the persevering as well as the brave—he can be of considerable use if he knows how to act.   If he stands still and uses his eyes he may see the fox approaching.   Then if a cur-dog—all dogs not hounds or terriers belonging to the pack are " cur-dogs " on hunting-days— courses the fox, or sheep-stain foils the scent and hounds inevitably check, he can go quietly forward if near enough, tell the huntsman what has happened and point out which way the fox travelled after the accident.   If he is too distant to do this he should endeavour to attract attention by holding up his head-gear, and only in the last resort should he holloa.   Before doing either he should get as near as possible to the place where he actually saw the fox, but without crossing its line: no one should ever cross the line of a fox until hounds have passed by.   To do otherwise would mean that hounds and huntsman might be drawn to a place where there was no scent, and much valuable time wasted.   It is to be remembered that hounds that have been taken to the holloa of a particular person two or three times and each time have hit off the scent, will learn to recognize that particular holloa, and to come to it without waiting for orders from their huntsman or rate from the whippers-in. Therefore it is well to be chary of holloaing and to stop others from holloaing, except in the last resort. I am afraid " the astonished traveller," " the listening ploughman," and " the distant shepherd " of Beckford by holloaing and running " to see him break " have throughout the ages done more to hinder sport than to forward it.

Be sure the fox you see is not only a fox—and not a hare or a collie-dog—but also the fox hounds are hunting, not a fresh fox. Otherwise you will only make matters worse by signalling his presence. When your observation and information have proved to be invariably accurate you may be honoured by a question from huntsman or master when hounds are brought to their noses. If you have *certain* information—knowledge acquired by means of your own eyes—give it by all means. But if you know nothing, not having seen anything, say so at once. Ignorance on a point of venery in a young sportsman is no disgrace : but to pretend you know when you are only guessing is a real crime, and will very soon lead to your presence in the hunting-field as a " foot-person " being cordially resented.

When a fox has been run to ground you may be of great use in running to the nearest farm-house or cottage for a pick or spade, or by holding one of the terriers. The same when a fox mysteriously disappears on the outskirts of a village, among farm-buildings, or the gardens and shrubberies surrounding a big house. A youngster's sharp eyes will frequently detect the fox crouching on a roof, or on an ivy-covered wall, or lurking in the rafters of a barn or outhouse. I once, when hounds threw up at the wall surrounding a village church-yard and had been held all round it without hitting-off the scent, remember noticing a number of old, hollow, flat-topped, box-shaped tombstones resting on side stones, and by striking matches discovering the fox inside one of them, having entered where the end stone had been broken away. There are, in fox-hunting, many similar occasions when a boy's unimpaired powers of observation may, properly utilized, prove of service to the hunt with which he goes out on foot.

Of course the foot-sportsman will be especially careful to avoid doing damage to other persons' property when following the hunt. He will not only be very careful not himself to break down fences, leave gates open, or cross fields of seeds or wheat, but will check other foot-people of his own age who may be inclined to offend, and set his elders an example to copy. The knowledge that someone sees them offending and can bear witness to the fact if questioned by the owner or occupier will insensibly act as a check upon the misdeeds of poachers, gypsies, loafers from adjoining towns and villages, and other undesirables, who under the pretence of following the hunt are really out to pick up such unconsidered trifles as a rabbit crouching in the dead bracken or among the roots. Sometimes, too, a labourer, discharged for some fault, will take the opportunity of surreptitiously and maliciously damaging the property of his late employer. The fact that someone is witness of his misdeed and may tell will act as a wholesome deterrent.

After the hunt has passed through, he can close and fasten the gate. If he sees a group of second-horsemen coming up—not under the control of a hunt-servant as these gentry ought always to be—larking and bucketing their masters' hunters about, in the knowledge they cannot be seen by them, he should always do so. If he replace a damaged rail in a fence he will earn the farmer's thanks, and if on his homeward way he find cattle astray upon the roads he should turn them into the nearest pasture-field and so secure both the cattle and their owner's gratitude as well as that of the master and officials of the hunt.

By behaving in this way the young sportsman will not only enjoy a full measure of sport, get healthy exercise and be of use to his brother-sportsmen, but will be storing up a real fund of knowledge against the time when he may be in a position to go a-hunting himself on something better than " Shanks, his mare."

Hare-Hunting

Much of what has been written concerning fox-hunting is, of course, applicable to the hunting of the hare ; but there are some differences which it will be well to point out.

In the first place there is little or no chance of the hunt, like a fox-chase, going straight away across country after a straight-necked quarry that precludes any chance of his seeing hounds again for the day, run he never so hardily. A hare-hunt usually takes place over the same large farm or group of small farms ; and when the ground has become foiled by the hunt passing over it several times a move is made merely to some adjoining unfoiled land. Hares run in rings, seldom travel away from the fields they customarily frequent, and when eventually driven out of their country run straight on for a limited distance and are then generally caught.

Whether the pack is one hunted and ridden to by mounted followers or followed entirely by a field on foot the above principles apply. In the former case the foot-sportsman's best plan is not to attempt to follow the field or riders ; but to mount any eminence in the centre of the ring described by the hunted hare and watch the sport from this coign of 'vantage. By so doing he will avoid adding to the damage caused, especially by a pack of harriers going over and over the same ground ; and may be able to render considerable assistance to the huntsman in times of difficulty.

A hunted hare will at first run up-hill rather than down, and if she turns left- (or right-)handed in the first instance will usually continue to turn in the same direction throughout the remainder of the hunt. The first thing, then, to notice after she has been found is the direction in which she first turns. Prior to the find the foot-sportsman may take a part in discovering

her as she sits in her " forme " in a furrow,
tussock of grass, under a whin-bush, or in a
hedge-bank. The mounted field will advance
in line behind the spreading pack, cracking their
crops to rouse the quarry : the farmers and
other foot-people will beat the hedges and thrust
their sticks or poles into any likely-looking
bush, bramble-brake, or bunch of gorse. Here the
novice must be careful to make no sign when
rabbits scuttle away in a hurry. Harriers are
nowadays often jealous hounds, fond of skirting
and staring about for help and holloas, depending
on the field to find them their quarry ; and not
all of them are broken from " bunnies." Even
when the hare has been seen squatting in her
" forme " it is better to hold up a cap as in fox-
hunting, and allow the master to decide whether
to give the pack a view, or to put her away
quickly ; and, when she has had sufficient " law,"
to lay them on the scent by drawing them carefully over her " forme " or the line she has just
taken.

When hounds are in full cry and the direction
of the first turn settled by the hare, the young
sportsman should act as before advised, get to
the centre of the probable circle whence he
may obtain a useful view of the hunt, and watch

for the return of puss to the place where she was found. He must be careful, of course, not to head her or turn her from her predestined circle ; but this is not difficult, as she is constantly looking backward as she runs, and unless he attracts her attention by moving, will rarely see him. It is quite sufficient if he will stand perfectly still the moment he views her approaching, even if he be in the middle of a bare, open pasture. In this case she will pass him undisturbed : may, indeed, actually run against his legs. To attempt concealment once she has been viewed, by stooping or crouching or hiding behind a hedge or tree, is fatal. The movement will inevitably attract her attention and she will be turned or perhaps headed.

If the sportsman remain motionless he will be able to get a near view and ascertain for certain whether she be a fresh hare or the hunted one. Also he will often have an opportunity of watching the remarkable manner in which she will endeavour to puzzle the pack instinctively by describing circles, returning on her own tracks, and finally with a sidelong jump flinging herself into a hedgerow or other place of refuge. Then when hounds come to the spot and can no longer hunt, the observer will be able to point out the place in which she is lying, and with a downward thrust of his stick send her flying out again, when the hunt will be resumed.

With packs of beagles or basset-hounds hunted and followed on foot, the foot-sportsman is, of course, actually inside his own kingdom. Nevertheless, unless he behaves as a true sportsman he will be as unwelcome there as he would anywhere else under similar conditions. He may take his place among the regular field now, and assist in the finding of the quarry; but there must be no noise or talking, for these little hounds are more liable to get their heads up even than harriers. When they begin to hunt he will take his place well behind the huntsman and whippers-in, and may then run as hard as he likes, provided he keeps in this position; and follow the line of the chase as a fox-hunter would. If he gets left behind there is absolutely no necessity for him to " pass through every field that hounds do," as I have known some super-conscientious lady-beaglers do. He may cut a corner here and there, and when he sees the pack has checked or killed, come up to them by the most direct route, and in this way avoid getting in the line of any fresh hare that may be started.

Beagling is one of the best sports to which

school-boys can be entered : indeed some of the most famous Masters of Foxhounds this country has produced owe the beginnings of their hunting knowledge to packs of foot-beagles. Some public schools and several colleges at both Universities maintain packs of beagles, and they are numerous in the neighbourhood of the Metropolis and of many large commercial and manufacturing centres, so that the younger men of the official, professional, and business classes can enjoy Saturday afternoon runs with them in the adjoining country without interfering with their regular avocations. In addition, many country squires before the war kept small packs of beagles to hunt over the land they owned and that of their immediate neighbours, and these proved a boon not only to the district, but also to the local masters of foxhounds.

The young sportsman, therefore, should, when hunting is finally restored to its pre-war condition, have very little difficulty in finding a pack with which he may run from time to time, to the great advantage of his health and to the advancement of his knowledge in many ways ; for, despite the faddists and puritans, there can be no better means of teaching him lessons that will, if applied, carry him usefully and successfully through life.

Otter-Hunting

This is a sport that can be enjoyed more freely by the young sportsman than most others, since it is pursued during precisely those months of late spring, summer, and early autumn that include the longest holiday periods. It is also a sport in the pursuit of which he can if uninstructed do more harm than almost any other. I must, therefore, direct his attention rather closely to the methods pursued in this sport, as they differ considerably from those belonging to any other kind of hunting.

The tyro at otter-hunting who has previously been out with foxhounds, harriers, and beagles will be a little bewildered when he attends his first meet of the otter-hounds. In the three latter sports the finding of the quarry is a small part of the proceedings : the chief thing being the gallop or run across country in the wake of the pack, so soon as the fox or hare has been set going. In otter-hunting the finding of the quarry is often the longest and most difficult part of the day's work ; and, except in the rare instances when a hunted otter takes to the land and makes a point for some well-known and more or less distant river or lake, there is never any running to be done.

K

When hounds are taken from the meeting-place to the waterside they first endeavour to hit off the " drag " or scent left by the otter among the aquatic herbage or on the sward of the water-meadows during its nocturnal journey up or down stream. When hounds strike the drag they open on it, and at the first notes of the pack the uninstructed too often start racing along the banks, overtake the hounds, over-run the drag and cause endless delay and confusion. When hounds are drawing, before they have found, and even if they are giving tongue all the while, the field should walk quietly and slowly along the banks ; and even when there is no drag and the pack is silent, should keep well behind the master and the huntsman. When hounds are working round a bend they should not take so short a cut across the meadow that they will reach the river at a spot in advance of the pack. There may be a line out into the meadow at any point, where an otter has been searching for frogs ; and if the field straggles over it in advance of hounds there will be very little chance of their puzzling out the line. Nothing can be gained by pressing upon hounds, for until the find there is nothing to see. Therefore walking and not running must be the order of the day when otter-hunting.

When hounds find, or " mark " at a holt, such as the roots of a tree or the exit of a drain on the river-bank, and the voices of the marking hounds prove that the quarry is at home, the field and especially the young sportsman who desires to prove his mettle, should stand still upon the bank exactly where he is when the mark takes place. He can see nothing and will only be in the way if he goes to the spot where hounds are marking. It may take a long time to move the quarry and force it to take to the water ; but when put down the field will be duly advertized of the fact by the master's horn or whistle, and by the " Tally-ho ! " of anyone who has seen the otter.

The hunt proper has now commenced and the field will have a chance of witnessing the sport— if they will only stand still. An otter usually takes a lot of hunting before it can be caught. It will swim both up and down the stream, under water, coming up in secure places to breathe, and it is the business of the pack to hunt it by the scent that, rising to the surface, floats upon the water, and of the field to assist hounds by signalling the presence of the otter near them should they chance to view it when it comes to the surface to " vent." Without such assistance it would take hounds a very long time to account for an average-sized otter in a moderate-sized stream. The duty, therefore, of every member of the field who aspires to be called a sportsman is, directly an otter is signalled as having been put down, to watch the water for signs of its presence, and if they are certain they see it, and are quite sure what they see is not a water-vole, a moor-hen, or a fish, to cry " Tally-ho ! " until the leading hounds have reached the spot and confirmed the observer's opinion by opening once more upon the scent.

The sportsman must be extremely careful not to " tally " anything that he is not sure is an otter : to do so is every bit as bad as to holloa a pack of foxhounds on a hare or a sheep-dog. He ought, therefore, to take the trouble to learn what an otter looks like, if he has never seen one in the flesh : either by studying the pictures in some Natural History Book, or by a visit to the Zoo-logial Gardens or a Natural History Museum. The best, and in fact the only, way to see an otter when it is in process of being hunted is to stand perfectly still upon the bank in a place where the observer can get a plain uninterrupted view of a stretch of water reaching from bank to bank, and to keep his eyes constantly fixed upon that stretch of water and no other.

Hounds will pass and re-pass, swimming the foil or hunting along the banks, the huntsman and whippers-in (and too often too many of the ignorant followers) will come and go, there will be tallies here and tallies there ; but let the young sportsman disregard them all, and never cease to watch the water, and he will be eventually—and generally when hounds are silent and all is quiet— rewarded by " viewing " the otter himself, and be able to shout " Tally-ho " and point with his pole to the exact spot at which it disappeared when he shouted. That should be one of the proudest moments of his sporting life, for he has proved himself a reliable " look-out "—above or below. Towards the end of a hunt, of course, if he is asked to come into the water and help to form a " stickle "—or line of men and women drawn across a shallow ford to prevent the quarry from going down stream into a deeper part of the river—he will leave his post on the bank and help in this office ; moving his pole gently from side to side as he sees the others do, to keep the otter from passing. But if the otter comes near him and he sees it he must be careful not to touch it with his pole or stick : as this is the worst crime that can be committed in the otter-hunting field, and one that he will never be forgiven.

During all this time, except when he has actually " gazed " the otter, he should keep silence. He should not chatter loudly as he marches along the bank when hounds are drawing; he should not talk or shout or call to friends across the river while he is watching the water ; and if anyone should so call to him the best rebuke he can make the offender is—without raising his eyes— to maintain perfect silence as though suddenly stricken stone-deaf. There will be plenty of opportunity for making a noise at the " worry," when hounds have caught their otter in midstream or on the bank, and again when it is broken-up and thrown to the pack.

There are sundry other ways in which the young sportsman may make himself useful in the otter-hunting field. In many packs not all the terriers are allowed to hunt with the pack until an otter has been marked, and some member of the field will be asked to lead them. This is a duty for which he may volunteer. As the little dogs will probably be very keen and inclined to strain at the lead and when young and not thoroughly entered, to show their anxiety to join in the sport by whining, the duty is not always one of the most pleasurable. A good master or considerate huntsman will realize this and

get someone to relieve the first volunteer after
a suitable interval. Terriers, too, are usually
picked up at a kill lest they should be mistaken
for the otter by the hounds when they are " seeing
red " ; and are then handed to some bystander
to be held until the quarry is broken up. Here
again the young sportsman may make himself
useful : as well as by going for spade or crowbar
to bolt an otter, or taking a message to the " look-
out below," or to the members of the hunt
forming a stickle, or to the man in charge of the
luncheon-cart on the road. The rules as to
damaging fences, shutting gates and walking
through growing crops—in the case of otter-
hunting these are represented chiefly by
" mowing-grass "—must be observed as in other
forms of hunting. The youthful sportsman will
always let hounds, hunt officials, and his seniors
precede him over or under stiles and obstacles ;
and, when barbed wire fences are to be crossed,
will be ready, by laying his pole or even his coat
along the top strand when taut, or lifting the
wire when slack, to assist any of the lady members
of the field to negotiate this abominable obstacle
without tearing their garments.

On the first occasion when he witnesses a kill
the master should " blood " him. This is done by

his taking a pad (or foot) and touching him
lightly on the forehead, cheeks, and chin with the
cut-off end, so as to leave a small stain of blood,
after which the pad will be presented to him,
and he can count himself entered to the sport.
His parents or guardians will not, it is to be
hoped, grudge the few shillings necessary to have
the pad preserved and mounted with a pin, so
that he may proudly wear it in his cap at sub-
sequent meets.

2. SHOOTING

There is quite a lot that a well-conducted boy
can do to make himself useful if he be allowed
to accompany the guns ; and at the same time,
is he goes in the proper spirit, quite a lot of
knowledge to be acquired that will stand him in
good stead when he has a gun of his own.

His earlier experience should be confined to
going out with one or two guns, possibly rabbit-
shooting or walking-up partridges in the roots
and stubbles. Here he will, in the first instance,
learn to keep silence, because the human voice
carries farther and has a more startling effect
on wild life than any other natural sound. He
will also learn to walk in line for safety's sake,
and if his mentors be safe shots, will, by observing

them closely, gain a knowledge of what to do and what to avoid doing when out shooting.

With his quickness of vision he can follow the flight of a wounded bird, and mark it down : can note the precise spot at which a towered bird fell : and so be of assistance in taking the retrievers or spaniels to the place where they may be most profitably set to work. He can also lead a dog that requires to be worked on a slip, carry a cartridge-bag, game-bag, or a frame to hold the birds, or the ferret-box when rabbiting, or even a luncheon-basket ; and by so doing prove his appreciation of the permission to accompany them accorded him by his elders.

During the day he will learn something of the habits of game : how to distinguish in September the immature pheasant that may not be shot, from the partridge that may: to detect the quail or the landrail that gets up before the guns : the leveret from the rabbit : even the thrush or field-fare from birds of game : and not to start or get excited when birds are flushed, but to stand silent and motionless until they are out of shot.

At the end of the day he may go to the gun-room and learn how guns should be cleaned and cared for : and if he is rewarded further by the gift of a brace of birds or a couple of rabbits to take home, neither he nor his mother is likely to think his day has been unprofitably spent.

Later on, perhaps, he may get the opportunity of a day with a bigger party of sportsmen, at driven pheasants or wild-duck, when he may be allowed to go with the guns or walk with the beaters. In either case there will be many things of interest for him to learn, and plenty of ways of making himself useful.

Or perhaps a father or an uncle will take him out for what is the best and most sportsmanlike form of entertainment with the gun : a day's rough-shooting; just the two of them and a single cocker-spaniel. The young sportsman will carry the game-bag, walking on the left-hand of the shooter, and the spaniel's business will be to find the game. Rough grass fields, furze commons, small spinneys with streams running through them, patches of marshy ground, hedge-rows full of berry-bearing bushes and ivy-covered trees will be beaten by the spaniel, his busy stump of a tail being the chief indication that he winds some sort of game ; unless it be a wood-cock, when a bell-like note should give timely warning of the bird he expects to flush.

In the variety of the sport lies its charm.

First a rabbit, perhaps, bolts from a tussock of grass and is rolled head over heels stone dead. Then with a prodigious fuss a cock-pheasant gets up out of a bramble-bush. A pair of old barren partridges next offer the chance of a right and left as they seek cover in the adjacent field of roots. The cocker's distinctive note gives warning just as the silent-winged woodcock glides from the holly-tree down the hedgerow, and turns abruptly over the top—clean missed with both barrels. Out of a swampy bit rises a wisp of snipe : the gunner waits while they scream and zig-zag, then drops one as he hangs for a second before going straight away down the wind. Out of the ivy-covered tree flies a pigeon ; the shot rattles on his quills, but he goes on unharmed. Another rabbit. A hare, in whose honour the sportsman quietly elevates the muzzle of his gun : as he does again immediately afterwards when a hen-pheasant rises.

Such are the varied shots and thrills afforded by a day's rough shooting ; and no more exciting or instructive way of entering a boy to sport with the gun can be conceived. But the shooter will not kill more than a couple or so of rabbits, if he be at all considerate of his youthful ghillie : since " bunnies " weigh heavy, and their weight increases in mathematical progression according to the distance they have to be carried.

The young sportsman who will cheerfully trudge by the side of his relative over rough ground and smooth, wet ground and dry, and carry the bag, speaking only when addressed, and willing to observe and learn all that he may, will deserve his lunch and some more substantial reward to enable him to pursue his own private hobby, than that almost sufficient in itself, of having enjoyed a day's genuine sport and seen game well-found and retrieved by a good dog, and killed dead in the air or clean missed by a humane and skilful shot.

3. COURSING

A big organized Coursing Meeting with its judge, slipper, stewards, flag-stewards, bookmakers, and crowds, is no place for the youthful sportsman : for its manifold excitements he must be content to wait until he is of riper age. There are still, however, owners and occupiers of land who rejoice in the old-fashioned sport of private coursing : men who, with perhaps a single greyhound or at most a couple, will go out over their own farms riding on a pony and with an attendant on foot to slip the dogs at a hare or a succession of hares, or will invite a coursing friend or neighbour to bring his own greyhounds and match them against those of his host.

If any such dwell in the district in which the young sportsman, for whom this book is chiefly written, happens to reside, he will find an opportunity of being allowed to take part in this very genuine form of the sport, and to prove himself useful in the coursing field. He may lead the dogs not in slips, carry the hares killed, and eventually be promoted to slip the greyhounds when a hare is started. His quick eyesight may, at other times, be useful in detecting the hare in her " forme," or with a pole or stick he may be able to put one out of a hedge or thicket of brambles.

In some districts the local farmers get up small coursing meetings for nominal sweepstakes, and although, perhaps, such meetings are not strictly held under National Coursing Club Rules, they are generally fair and sportsmanlike events, properly carried out, with a mounted judge, a slipper, and a few stewards equipped with flags of the proper colours : although there will be no printed programmes and no " bookies."

Here, too, the young sportsman may profitably take a part in helping to show good sport. The hares will be walked-up by the crowd, having in front of it the slipper with his brace of competing dogs, accompanied by the judge on his cob. Perhaps he may be entrusted with one of the green flags carried at each end of the formed line to mark the point on either hand, beyond which the spectators may not be allowed to straggle, lest they disturb ground reserved for trials later in the day. Or he may act as flag-steward, his duty being to hoist the red or white flag denoting the winner in a tie, according to the handkerchief of one of these colours waved by the judge after a decided course : or the yellow or blue flags employed to denote a " bye " or an " undecided." He can hold the sheets of the dogs in slips, or the red and white woollen collars used when both competitors are of the same colour ; carry the bottles of liniment or stimulant with which greyhounds are rubbed and dosed after their courses, and learn how to pick up a dog after a kill, rub him over, clothe him and lead him about until his next tie is run off.

It will be seen that there are many minor ways in which a boy who possesses the sporting instinct may participate in the day's amusement and be of real use and value to the owners of the greyhounds engaged, and the officials of the meeting ; while, at the same time, assimilating practical knowledge of the Rules of Coursing and of the correct way to conduct the sport, against the time when he may be in a position to assume himself the rôle of Public Courser.

4. ANGLING

Angling has always possessed an overpowering attraction for most boys, although it is to be feared that from many different causes a majority eventually outgrows the love of catching fish by means of " a piece of string and a bent pin." One of these is undoubtedly the lack of encouragement shown them by their elders, especially in strictly-preserved water, where the trout and grayling-fishing is highly rented and there is no " public fishing " to be obtained.

An angler who is also a sportsman—which is by no means invariably the case in these days of syndicates and war-profiteers—can do much to cultivate the budding taste of the young sportsman, even in preserved water, by taking him with him to the riverside and showing him how fish are to be caught by rod and line in a fair and legitimate manner.

If his elder be a bottom-fisherman it may be that the sport will prove a little dull to the boy

of active habit of mind and body ; but if he be
a fly-fisherman intent on catching trout or
grayling, dace or chub with the artificial imita-
tion of the natural fly, his day will be full of
interest and excitement, and there will be much
for him to learn.

The putting together of rod, reel, and line,
the fitting of the cast, the choice of flies, are but
the absorbing preliminaries to the actual casting
of the lure over a rising fish, the striking, playing,
and eventually landing of it, the killing it, and
laying it in the creel, lined with damp meadow-
grass to preserve its freshness and beauty for as
long as may be.

After he has witnessed the capture of a few
fish by an expert angler he may be allowed to take
a more active part and given the landing-net to
manipulate at the proper moment. To place
this under the hooked fish in the proper way and
at the correct time requires some practice ; but
when he lifts his first one-pounder skilfully to
the bank his joy will be supreme ; and, given a
fair opportunity by the Fates, he will remain an
angler at heart ever after.

Besides landing his fish for the successful
angler who is giving him his day on the river or
stream, the young sportsman can make himself

useful in various ways. He can carry the creel
or bag, the waterproof or waders, the gaff or
landing-net,as the case may be. When the angler's
fly gets caught up, as it will from time to time,
in grass or weed behind him, in tree or bush above
or below, he can come gaily to the rescue and be
of much help in releasing the fly. When the
lure is caught in the bed of the stream he can,
if it be not too deep, wade in and save a break ;
or hold the rod while its owner does so. Or he
can make the " wreath " of willow, bent into the
form of a hoop just big enough to slip over the
butt of the rod and the reel, which, being sent
down the line into the water, will often cause the
caught-up hook to come safely away.

Then again, there is the frequent case of a
tangled cast, or of the line twisted round the
rod-top. Here the young sportsman can be of
incalculable use to his patron, by clearing the
line from the end-ring in the latter instance, and
by carefully disentangling the gut-cast from the
knots and loops, into which it is capable of getting
itself so mysteriously twisted at a second's
notice. When fish are on the feed, the angler's
best plan, if accompanied by an intelligent youth,
is to cut it off, attach another and go on fishing,
leaving his brother-sportsman—for such he is

L

entitled to be called—to unravel the mess quietly
and at leisure on the bank. Not every angler
is so young as he would like to be, nor is his
eyesight always very good, and a boy who can
attach a fly nimbly to a gut point with a Turle
knot, is sure to be valued as a sportsman and
companion, and taught many things that it
would take him years to learn as the result of
experience laboriously acquired by himself.

In conclusion, I will merely add that, to whichever of the Major Field Sports such a youthful
sportsman as I have had in my mind's eye while
writing these pages, may be admitted as spectator
or participant, he should endeavour not only to
learn and strictly to observe the rules; but also
to make himself useful to those who are con-
ducting the particular sport of the moment.
In this way his presence will be welcomed rather
than tolerated: he will feel " one of them " himself:
will store up invaluable lessons for the future;
and, above all, will earn for himself a reputation
that will carry him very far in any walk in life that
may subsequently fall to his lot.

One may be born rich or poor, a gentleman or
a peasant, an artist or an artizan ; but it is within
the power of any boy to earn for himself the title
most worth having in this world, and one,

lacking which, all others are comparatively worthless—that of being a Sportsman, in the truest and most genuine sense of the word.

INDEX

164

PRINTED BY THE ANCHOR PRESS LTD. TIPTREE, ESSEX, ENGLAND.

Printed in the United States
23004LVS00001B/376-423